# Ancient Civilizations

*An Enthralling Journey Through the Great Societies of the Ancient World, Including Mesopotamia, Egypt, the Indus Valley, and Beyond*

© Copyright 2025 - All rights reserved.

The content contained within this book may not be reproduced, duplicated, or transmitted without direct written permission from the author or the publisher.

Under no circumstances will any blame or legal responsibility be held against the publisher, or author, for any damages, reparation, or monetary loss due to the information contained within this book, either directly or indirectly.

### Legal Notice:

This book is copyright protected. It is only for personal use. You cannot amend, distribute, sell, use, quote, or paraphrase any part, or the content within this book, without the consent of the author or publisher.

### Disclaimer Notice:

Please note the information contained within this document is for educational and entertainment purposes only. All effort has been executed to present accurate, up-to-date, reliable, and complete information. No warranties of any kind are declared or implied. Readers acknowledge that the author is not engaging in the rendering of legal, financial, medical, or professional advice. The content within this book has been derived from various sources. Please consult a licensed professional before attempting any techniques outlined in this book.

By reading this document, the reader agrees that under no circumstances is the author responsible for any losses, direct or indirect, that are incurred as a result of the use of the information contained within this document, including, but not limited to, errors, omissions, or inaccuracies.

# Free limited time bonus

Stop for a moment. We have a free bonus set up for you. The problem is this: we forget 90% of everything that we read after 7 days. Crazy fact, right? Here's the solution: we've created a printable, 1-page pdf summary for this book that you're reading now. All you have to do to get your free pdf summary is to go to the following website: https://livetolearn.lpages.co/enthrallinghistory/

Or, Scan the QR code!

Once you do, it will be intuitive. Enjoy, and thank you!

# Table of Contents

INTRODUCTION .................................................................................... 1
CHAPTER 1: THE DAWN OF CIVILIZATION ................................. 2
CHAPTER 2: THE SPLENDOR OF ANCIENT EGYPT .................. 13
CHAPTER 3: THE INDUS VALLEY .................................................. 25
CHAPTER 4: THE MYSTERIES OF THE MINOANS AND MYCENAEANS .................................................................................... 35
CHAPTER 5: ANCIENT CHINA— FROM XIA TO ZHOU ............ 48
CHAPTER 6: THE RISE OF THE HITTITES AND THE ASSYRIANS ........... 59
CHAPTER 7: THE PERSIAN EMPIRE ............................................. 72
CHAPTER 8: THE GOLDEN AGE OF CLASSICAL GREECE ...... 84
CHAPTER 9: ANCIENT ROME ......................................................... 95
CONCLUSION ................................................................................... 105
HERE'S ANOTHER BOOK BY ENTHRALLING HISTORY THAT YOU MIGHT LIKE ............................................................................ 107
FREE LIMITED TIME BONUS ........................................................ 108
BIBLIOGRAPHY ............................................................................... 109
IMAGE SOURCES ............................................................................. 112

# Introduction

What comes to mind when you think of the world's most influential ancient civilizations? This book explores nine ancient cultures that left a lasting legacy. How did they begin? What stunning cultural, technological, and societal innovations did they contribute? How did writing, government, religion, architecture, and other aspects make each civilization stand out? These civilizations gave us the first writing, the first alphabet, the first transportation wheel, the first beer, the first law codes, the first cities, the first mathematics, the first Olympic games, the first republic, and much more.

Did you know people were grinding grain into flour and baking bread at least seven thousand years ago? By approximately 5000 BCE, bread had become a staple food in Mesopotamia. Why did Egypt's first "real" pyramid collapse before its completion? How did Greece lose its written language and most of its major cities? This book will keep you turning pages as it reveals the stories of these exceptional civilizations.

These ancient societies had to adapt to their environment and deal with harsh climate change. They were not islands to themselves. These civilizations all interacted with neighboring cultures through trade, marriage, and yes, warfare.

The spellbinding histories of how these ancient civilizations changed the world are compelling. Their stories help us understand why things are the way they are today in every aspect of our lives. Let's travel back in time and around the globe to learn their breathtaking tales.

# Chapter 1:
# The Dawn of Civilization

The Ubaid and Sumerian civilizations introduced an awe-inspiring number of "firsts" to our world. These cultures blossomed in southern Mesopotamia—the "land between the rivers." Most of Mesopotamia (today's Iraq, eastern Syria, and sections of Turkey, Saudi Arabia, Kuwait, and Iran) lay between the Tigris and Euphrates rivers. Mesopotamia, "the Cradle of Civilization," stretched

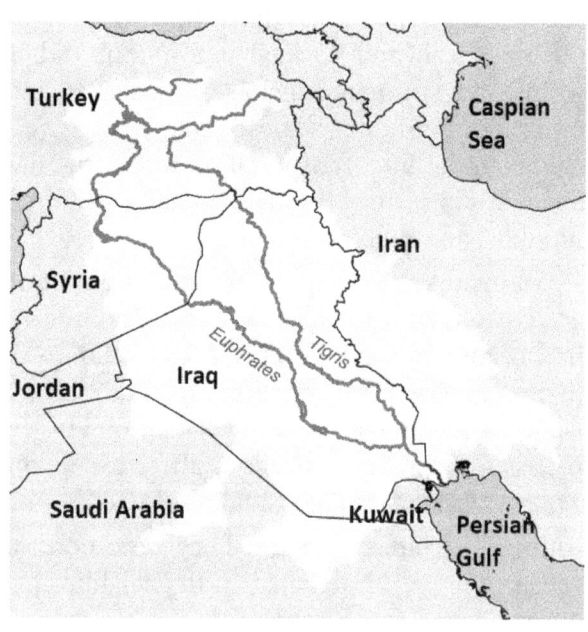

Mesopotamia covers the light area of this map. [1]

from the headwaters of the Euphrates and Tigris to where the rivers joined and emptied into the Persian Gulf.

Around 6500 BCE, the Ubaid culture, a precursor to the Sumerians, emerged in southern Mesopotamia. This civilization may have been related to the Hassuna and Samarra cultures of central and northern

Mesopotamia. The people of the Ubaid civilization migrated south with their cattle, goats, and sheep, eventually reaching the Persian Gulf coast.

They exchanged their tents for reed-thatched huts and settled in villages. By 5500 BCE, they learned to make sun-dried mud bricks to build sturdy houses with flat roofs and arched doorways. The people of the Ubaid culture made clay ovens for baking bread and firing distinctive pottery with linear artwork. The rivers, lakes, and gulf were rich sources of seafood. By 5200 BCE, they built small boats (some with sails) to ply the waterways, even sailing down the Persian Gulf.

An Ubaid pottery jar, circa 5000 BCE [a]

They made their tools and weapons from stone, flint, or obsidian (a type of volcanic glass). Initially, they consumed wild grains, but later they began cultivating barley, emmer wheat, flax, and lentils. From these grains, they made beer, porridge, and bread. By 4500 BCE, they were weaving linen cloth from the flax fibers.

The people of the Ubaid civilization built Eridu, perhaps the world's oldest city, around 5400 BCE. The *Sumerian King List* states that it was the first city to hold "kingship" over the region before the Great Flood swept over.[1] At least two other contenders vie for "first city" status:

---

[1] Sumerian King List, trans. Jean-Vincent Scheil, Stephen Langdon, and Thorkild Jacobsen (Livius, updated 2020). https://www.livius.org/sources/content/anet/266-the-sumerian-king-list/#Translation.

Jericho (in today's West Bank), built about 8000 BCE, and Çatalhöyük (in today's Turkey), built around 7100 BCE. Yet, both settlements lacked the infrastructure that typically defines a city, such as roads and public buildings.

During the Ubaid period, Eridu covered an area of approximately twenty-five acres, with a population of around four thousand people. It had roads, a one-room temple, and other infrastructure. Eridu's irrigation system for crops, using ditches and canals, was probably the world's oldest. Irrigation was a game-changer, enabling agricultural productivity that could feed thousands in a dry climate.

Around 5000 BCE, the people of the Ubaid culture built the city of Ur at the mouth of the Euphrates, twelve miles east of Eridu. They also built Uruk on the Euphrates, about fifty-eight miles north of Ur. Uruk and Ur were chief cities of incredible wealth for the Ubaid culture and later the Sumerians.

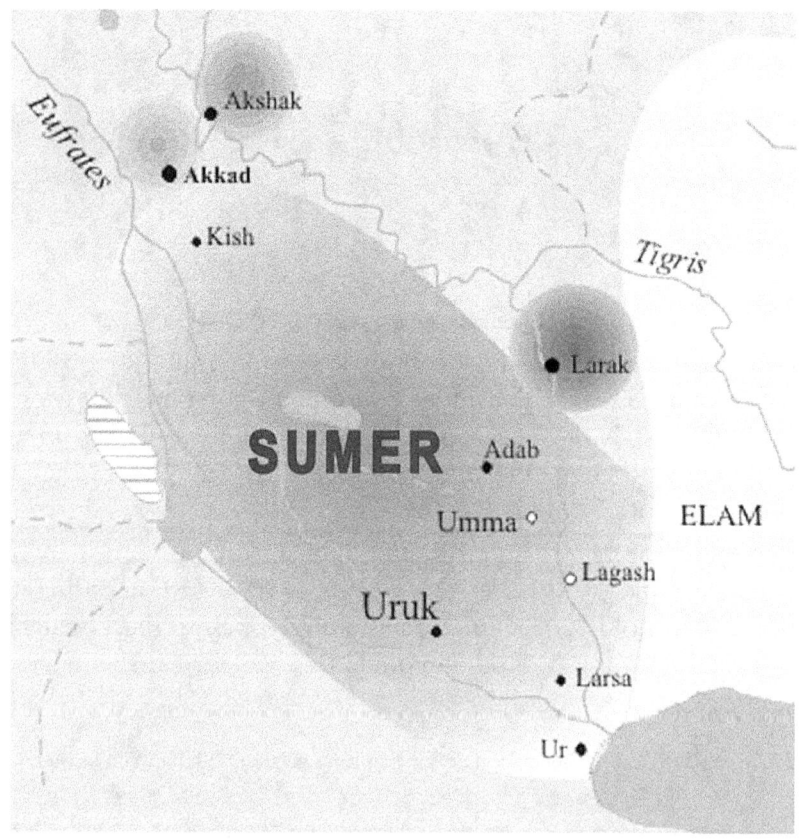

Dominant cities of the Ubaid and Sumerian civilizations [8]

The Ubaid civilization abandoned Ur and Eridu between 3800 and 3500 BCE. Ur suffered a catastrophic flood caused by the rising water levels of the Persian Gulf, which disrupted the Euphrates River delta. Changing weather patterns led to devastating droughts and sandstorms. Eridu depended on Lake Hammar, adjacent to the city, for irrigation. However, drought made the lake's water saline. Without a water source, Eridu became a ghost town, covered by the blowing sand.

By contrast, Uruk thrived thanks to its irrigation canals connected to the Euphrates. Uruk was Mesopotamia's powerhouse in this era, characterized by a hierarchical social system, a well-developed military, pottery factories, and full-time administrative officials. The city may have taken in refugees from Ur and Eridu, as its population grew exponentially in this era.

However, the Sumerians were migrating into southern Mesopotamia and may have driven Uruk's sudden population growth. They called themselves the "black-haired people" and spoke a language isolate unrelated to any other known language. They adopted many aspects of the Ubaid civilization, to the point that some scholars think the Sumerians were an extension of the Ubaid culture. Yet, the Sumerians possessed new skills, such as sophisticated metalworking. If they were from somewhere else, possibly Iran or northern Mesopotamia, the Sumerians peacefully assimilated.

The Sumerians introduced incredible innovations. The growing cities needed taxes for things like building and maintaining the irrigation canals and the city walls. Everyone paid a "tax," usually of fish or grain. Yet, the administrators needed a way to keep track of the numbers. The Sumerians used a sexagesimal counting system, counting in sets of twelve and sixty. Instead of counting fingers, they counted their twelve finger joints on the four fingers of one hand. When they reached twelve, they held up one finger on the other hand and started counting again. After counting to twelve again, they held up a second finger.

Twelve joints on one hand multiplied by five fingers on the other hand came to sixty. This numerical system brought us the twelve-hour day and night, the sixty-second minute, and the sixty-minute hour. The Sumerians used little cones and balls made from clay to keep track of higher numbers before they invented writing. A small cone stood for one, a small ball represented ten, and a larger cone represented sixty.

Pictographs from Uruk, late fourth millennium [4]

By 3500 BCE, the ground-breaking Sumerians used cut reeds to draw circles (for the "ten" ball), triangles (for the "sixty" cone), and other shapes into soft clay. The clay hardened into small tablets that preserved the world's first accounting system. By 3300 BCE, the Sumerians in Uruk developed proto-cuneiform writing using simple pictographs.

Over the next several centuries, the pictographs evolved into more abstract forms, incorporating the wedge-shaped symbols characteristic of logographic cuneiform writing. Each symbol represented a word or a word part. Since the Sumerians wrote on soft clay that hardened, thousands of Sumerian tablets have survived. Cuneiform writing was later used by the Babylonians, Assyrians, and other cultures.

Sumerian cuneiform, circa 2600 BCE [5]

By 3500 BCE, the Sumerians learned that heating copper and tin alloy to high temperatures produced bronze. This revolutionized warfare and farming, since bronze is a hard metal. Plows with bronze tips cut the soil more effectively, enhancing agricultural output and contributing to population growth. Bronze armor and shields were lighter than copper yet stronger against arrows and swords.

A key element of Sumerian history and literature was the Great Flood. The *Sumerian King List* divides the history of their cities and kings into two periods: before and after the flood. The Sumerian *Eridu Genesis* and *The Epic of Gilgamesh* tell the story of the flood. In the *Eridu Genesis*[2], the gods created the dark-haired people and the animals. They handed heaven's scepter to Eridu, giving its kings authority over all the people. However, the people were noisy as they worked in the canals and fields. The gods could not sleep with the hubbub. Highly irritated, the god Enlil persuaded the other gods to destroy the people. Yet, the god Enki quietly made plans to save the humans.

At that time, Ziusudra was the king and priest of Eridu. One day, while he stood in Eridu's shrine, he heard a voice from the other side of the wall. It was Enki. "Step up to the wall and listen!" he said. "The gods have decided to destroy mankind. The command of An and Enlil cannot be revoked. A flood will sweep over the cities."

At this point in the narrative, the *Eridu Genesis* tablet is damaged, but the *Epic of Gilgamesh*[3] picks up the story as told by Utnapishtim (another name for Ziusudra). The god Ea (Enki) told Utnapishtim, "Tear down your house and build a boat! Abandon your possessions and save your family and the animals. Make them all go into the boat."

So Utnapishtim built the boat and brought his family and the animals onto it. A black cloud arose from the horizon and covered the land. A torrent of rain fell so heavily that no one could see their hand in front of their face. Water submerged the mountains and covered the people. The goddess Ishtar (Inanna) shrieked and wailed at the devastation. The rest of the gods wept with her, regretting the catastrophe.

---

[2] *Eridu Genesis*, trans. Thorkild Jacobson (Livius, last updated 2020). https://www.livius.org/sources/content/oriental-varia/eridu-genesis/.
[3] *The Epic of Gilgamesh*, trans. N. K. Sandars (London: Penguin Classics, 1960).

For six days and seven nights, the storm pounded, and the flood writhed like a woman in labor. On the seventh day, all was quiet. As the sun came out, Utnapishtim fell to his knees, weeping. He scanned the horizon for land. Finally, he saw the tip of Mount Nimush emerging from the water. The boat lodged on the mountain, and, after seven days, Utnapishtim released a dove. It flew away but returned because it could find no place to perch. He released a swallow, and it also came back. Then he released a raven. By this time, the water had slithered off the land, and the raven did not return.

Utnapishtim came out of the boat, butchered oxen and sheep, and offered a sacrifice to the gods. Enlil was furious that some humans had survived, but Enki (Ea) intervened. Enlil sent the surviving humans to live at the mouth of the rivers (the Euphrates and Tigris—or southern Mesopotamia).

*The Epic of Gilgamesh* says that Utnapishtim told his story to Gilgamesh, the king of Uruk. He was still alive in Gilgamesh's day because the gods granted him immortality. Several ancient documents list Gilgamesh as a king of Uruk in the twenty-seventh century BCE, when Uruk held "kingship" or dominance over the other cities of southern Mesopotamia.

Uruk was the largest city in the world at that time, with a population exceeding fifty thousand. It had a forty-foot-high ziggurat—a rectangular sloping or stepped tower. Uruk's Anu ziggurat had the White Temple at its top. Uruk had jaw-dropping wealth because of its strategic location on the Euphrates River. Its river traffic made it a dominant trade hub, and irrigation from the river enabled the cultivation of lush farms.

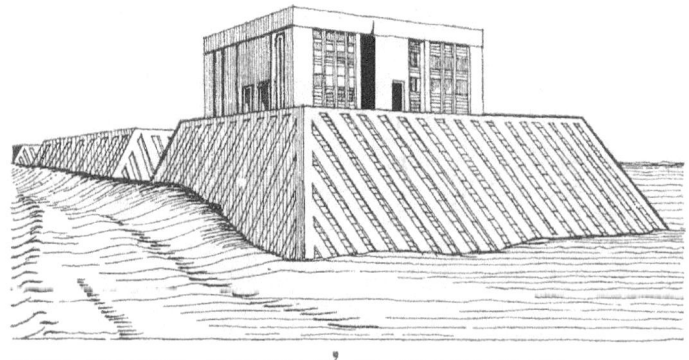

A drawing of Uruk's White Temple ziggurat⁶

Because writing had not been invented yet, by the sixth millennium, the Ubaid civilization used stamp seals to "sign" their names. Stamp seals were square or circular stones, approximately one inch in diameter, with a design carved into their surface. When pressed into a ball of soft clay, the clay hardened to preserve the design. Most men (and some women) had their own unique seal. The small disks of hardened clay indicated ownership of the materials they bought and sold.

Uruk took the idea of stamp seals up a notch by inventing cylinder seals around 3500 BCE. These were stone or metal cylinders, about four inches long. As with the stamp seals, each cylinder seal had a unique design, but the carving could be more complex because they were larger. The cylinder seal's owner rolled it in soft clay to leave an impression that hardened. Men and women wore cylinder seals hanging on lanyards around their necks or pinned to their clothing.

Uruk's Lady of Warka mask [7]

The "Lady of Warka" mask found in Uruk was carved from marble around 3100 BCE. It is the world's first known realistic depiction of a human face. Earlier artwork showed bizarre distortions of the face. For instance, the Ubaid "lizard-lady" statuettes, dating to around 4000 BCE, featured normal women's bodies but reptilian faces. Scholars believe the Lady of Warka mask represented Inanna, Uruk's patron goddess.

The Sumerians rebuilt Ur around 3500 BCE, and it grew to a population of around 34,000. Ur developed into an incredibly wealthy city, as seen with the fortune buried in Queen Puabi's tomb about 2600 BCE. Puabi's headdress, weighing over six pounds, had wreaths of gold leaf, beads of carnelian and lapis lazuli, and a gold comb. Her silver chariot was buried with her, along with over a hundred servants and soldiers, who were sacrificed to serve her in the afterlife.

By 2900 BCE, the weather patterns had improved, and the Sumerians rebuilt Eridu. They erected a temple called the House of Aquifer to worship Eridu's patron god, Enki, who ruled the underground water. Over time, the Sumerians enlarged the temple until it was probably the largest Sumerian ziggurat.

Initially, Sumerian kings held the title of "ensi," which meant they held a dual role as both priest and king. As the Sumerian cities grew, the king focused more on secular affairs, such as supervising builders, farmers, fishermen, herders, and merchants. The king's title changed to "lugal" or "strongman," since he was the military's commander-in-chief and the law's chief justice. A hereditary class of priests offered sacrifices, discerned omens, and performed other religious duties.

The Sumerians worshiped many gods and goddesses. The top three gods were An, Enki, and Enlil. An (Anu) was heaven's supreme god. Enki (Ea) was the god of the earth, aquifers, and healing. He protected humans when the other gods wanted to kill them. Enlil ruled the wind and atmosphere. Inanna (Ishtar) was Uruk's patron deity and the goddess of beauty, love, sex, and war. Her twin brother, Utu, was the sun god. Enlil's son, Nanna (Sin), was the moon god.

The Sumerians thought they existed to serve the gods. Failure to appease the gods led to floods, droughts, or enemy invasions. The Sumerians prayed daily, offered incense, sang hymns, and asked for forgiveness for their sins. When they prayed, they kneeled, lay face down on the ground, or stood with their arms lifted in the air or with one hand in front of their mouth.

The world's first known wheel was a potter's wheel developed in Iran around 5200 BCE. The Sumerians adopted the potter's wheel by 3100 BCE. Then, they realized they could use it for something else—transportation! These trailblazers invented the world's first rotating axle and built the first carts. Then, they had the bright idea of using animals to pull their carts, so they developed the world's first collars for donkeys and oxen that connected to a pole, which attached to the cart. The Sumerians also invented breeching straps.

Initially, they probably used wheeled carts for hauling things. Then, they developed four-wheeled chariots pulled by four kungas (a cross between a donkey and a wild ass). The first chariots were slow and awkward, but mosaics in a wooden box called the Standard of Ur (circa 2600 BCE) show the Sumerians trampling the enemy with their kunga-drawn chariots.

The kungas pulling the front chariot mow down a victim in this Standard of Ur mosaic.'

By 2600 BCE, the ingenious Sumerians used multiplication, division, basic geometry, cubic roots, and square roots. By 2300 BCE, they invented a stone abacus using divisions of one, ten, sixty, six hundred, and thirty-six hundred. Instead of beads on rods, like the Chinese version, theirs had columns with tiny stones.

The Sumerians developed a calendar system around 3100 BCE consisting of twelve lunar months in a year. Each month had twenty-nine or thirty days. A new month began when the slender crescent of a new moon appeared in the sky. However, twelve lunar months were only 354 days, while the solar year was about 365 days. To fix the problem, they occasionally added an extra month.

In addition to developing the world's first writing system, the Sumerians probably wrote the world's first story, the *Epic of Gilgamesh*. We already delved into the flood story part of the epic, but its overall theme was the quest for immortality. Gilgamesh was the flawed king of Uruk, disliked by his citizens. They used a prostitute to tame a wild man named Enkidu, who lived in the wilderness, and brought him to Uruk to challenge their king.

Gilgamesh and Enkidu fought until they were worn out. They realized they were evenly matched and decided it was better to be friends than foes. They set off together on an adventure to kill the sacred Humbaba monster that guarded the cedars of Lebanon. After killing the monster, they made a raft and sailed down the Euphrates back to Uruk. However, the goddess Inanna, patron of Uruk, saw Gilgamesh bathing and was enchanted by his stunning good looks.

"Marry me!" cried Inanna. Yet, Gilgamesh was uninterested.

Inanna flew to her father, Anu, the supreme god. "I want the Bull of Heaven!"

Anu hesitated, but Inanna screamed, "If you don't give it to me, I'll unleash the zombies from the underworld on the living!"

Inanna took the Bull of Heaven to Uruk. When the bull snorted, the ground collapsed into a pit, swallowing the people. Enkidu grabbed the bull by the horns, and Gilgamesh stabbed and killed the sacred animal. However, that got them in trouble with heaven. The gods decided that one man must die for killing the two divine creatures: the Humbaba and the Bull of Heaven. Although Gilgamesh had killed both animals, the gods did not want to disrupt Uruk's kingship, so they killed Enkidu instead. Gilgamesh wept for days over his friend.

Enkidu's death reminded him that he would also die one day. Gilgamesh set off on a quest, searching for Utnapishtim, who had become immortal. Utnapishtim gave Gilgamesh tasks to become young again, but Gilgamesh failed. The king of Uruk finally realized that his mortal body would die, yet by becoming a superior king, his memory would live on forever.

In 2334 BCE, Sargon, king of Kish, united the Akkadian tribes of northern Mesopotamia. They invaded the Sumerians, taking city by city, and established the Akkadian Empire, which ruled Mesopotamia until 2154 BCE. Raids from the Gutian mountain people undid the Akkadian Empire, along with the 4.2-kiloyear BP aridification event, a horrific drought that turned the grassy plains into deserts.

The Sumerians survived because they used irrigation farming, while the Akkadians were primarily herders, now with no grass for their flocks. Sumer's population even doubled as Akkadian and Amorite herders migrated south. The Sumerians staged a comeback with the Third Dynasty of Ur (2112-2004 BCE). Ur was now the largest city in the world, with sixty-five thousand people. Their king, Ur-Nammu, wrote the world's first law code. Yet, in 2004 BCE, the brilliant dynasty fell to the raiding Elamites from Iran.

Imprint from a cylinder seal dedicated to Ur-Nammu <sup>9</sup>

# Chapter 2:
# The Splendor of Ancient Egypt

Ancient Egypt's magnificent civilization flourished along the life-giving waters of the Nile River. How did the Egyptians harness the Nile's resources? What can we learn from its architectural marvels, advanced knowledge, and rich cultural heritage? This chapter unwraps a complex society marked by towering pyramids, spectacular temples, a sophisticated writing system, and profound religious beliefs.

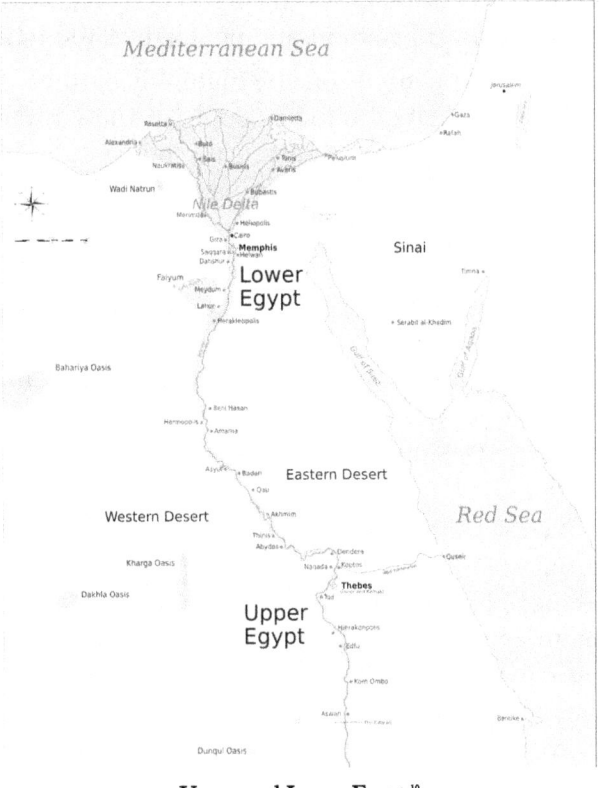

Upper and Lower Egypt [10]

Egypt's story revolves around the Nile River, its source of life. Curiously, northern Egypt is called "Lower Egypt," and southern Egypt is referred to as "Upper Egypt." Why? The Nile flows north from its southern highlands to the flat delta region in the north, where the river splits into multiple tributaries before emptying into the Mediterranean Sea.

While 92 percent of Egypt is desert, the Nile Delta is lush and green. The Nile's annual flooding deposits rich silt, which fertilizes the land. The delta had grasslands for herds and fertile soil for farming. The Nile's predictable flooding cycles also enabled agriculture along the riverbanks south of the delta. Although Egypt gets less rainfall than any other country, most years its people could depend on the Nile to irrigate their farms.

Around 3400 BCE, in the Predynastic period (4300–3100 BCE), the ancient Egyptians began building towns and cities, using sun-dried bricks. Xois was on an island in the delta region and later became one of Egypt's capitals. The town of Nekhen (Hierakonpolis) in Upper Egypt grew to at least five thousand people by 3400 BCE.

The Egyptian custom of mummifying their dead had begun by this time. At first, they buried people in the scorching desert sands, which naturally dried and preserved the bodies. By 3350 BCE, the Egyptians began using embalming agents like pine resin, plant extracts, and bitumen, a form of petroleum.

Trade began between Egypt and southern Mesopotamia in the Ubaid era. The Egyptians treasured beads made from the dazzling, deep-blue lapis lazuli stone. The Ubaid and Sumerian people acquired lapis lazuli from long-distance trade with Afghanistan, then traded it to Egypt. Through interacting with the Sumerians, the Egyptians began using cylinder seals by 3300 BCE. Their favorite stone for the seal was lapis lazuli.

People settled in Abydos, Upper Egypt, by at least 3500 BCE. The people of Abydos began writing pictographs around 3400 BCE. Some pictographs represented the object in the picture, but others represented another word that sounded like the noun in the picture. As with the ancient Sumerians, the Egyptians used pictographs for record-keeping in their early days. By 3200 BCE, the pictographs were evolving into hieroglyphics. Despite the robust trade between Egypt and Mesopotamia, Egyptian hieroglyphics were distinctive from Sumerian cuneiform.

Abydos pictographs [11]

The ability to read Egyptian hieroglyphics was lost after centuries of Roman rule over Egypt. However, scholars finally unlocked the mysterious language in the early 1800s CE after an ancient monument was unearthed that honored the coronation of a new Greek pharaoh. Alexander the Great's general, Ptolemy I, began Egypt's Ptolemaic dynasty in 305 BCE. Ptolemy's descendant, the fourteen-year-old Ptolemy V, became Egypt's pharaoh in 196 BCE. The Egyptian priests recorded the event with the Rosetta Stone, which had the same inscription written in three different languages: Greek, Egyptian hieroglyphics, and Egyptian Demotic (which emerged around 700 BCE). In 1799 CE, Napoleon's army discovered the polished black granodiorite stone. This was an exciting find because scholars could read the Greek inscription and then translate the Egyptian hieroglyphics and Demotic script from that. It unlocked Egypt's history, including its early rulers.

At the beginning of the Early Dynastic era (3100-2700 BCE), King Narmer ("Stinging Catfish") rose to power in Upper Egypt. (Egyptians did not call their rulers "pharaoh" until the New Kingdom.) King Narmer unified Upper and Lower Egypt into one kingdom, celebrating his triumph with a two-foot-high stone monument called the Narmer Palette. One side of the slab shows Narmer grasping the hair of a kneeling captive and swinging a mace with the other hand. This motif became common in Egyptian victory monuments. The other side of the stone slab has two serpopards (long-necked leopards) intertwining their necks, representing the union of southern and northern Egypt.

**A drawing of the conjoined serpopards from the Narmer Palette** [12]

Not only did Narmer unite Egypt, but he also expanded into the Sinai Peninsula, Gaza, and Canaan (today's Israel and Palestine). Pottery and seals with his name have been found throughout these regions. His brilliant reign ended with a deadly attack by a hippopotamus. (Even today, hippopotamuses kill twice as many people in Africa as lions.)

Four centuries later, the Old Kingdom, also known as the Age of the Pyramids, dawned (2700–2200 BCE). Egyptologists organize Egypt's ancient history into three "kingdoms" that they consider golden ages: the Old Kingdom, the Middle Kingdom, and the New Kingdom. These periods had high-powered kings who stimulated prosperity and exciting new developments. "Intermediate periods" of chaotic politics and economic downturns came between the three kingdoms.

Manetho, a third-century BCE Egyptian-Greek historian and priest, attempted to organize Egypt's long history into dynasties in which a single family, or sometimes an ethnic group, held power for a significant period. Often, two or three dynasties ruled different parts of Egypt simultaneously. Scholars squabble over when these kingdoms and dynasties began and ended, so dates in this chapter try to strike a middle ground.

King Djoser, the first king of the Old Kingdom, reunited Egypt again and built the first pyramid. His was a step pyramid, a precursor to the smooth-sided, pointy-topped pyramids typically associated with Egypt. Djoser's pyramid was an extended mastaba, a rectangular building about twenty feet high with a flat roof and sloping walls. Egyptians buried a dead person under the mastaba in a tomb at the bottom of a shaft. A second shaft led to a storage room next to the tomb for things the person needed in the afterlife, such as food, beer, games, and clothing. The Pyramid of Djoser in Saqqara had underground shafts, but instead of a single level above ground, it has six levels, each slightly smaller, rising 204 feet high.

King Djoser's pyramid in Saqqara[18]

Most of Egypt's pyramids were built during the Old Kingdom. The kings who followed Djoser employed thousands of workers and spent a fortune building higher and grander pyramids. Egypt did not have the wheel yet, so workers had to drag the massive stones on enormous sleds over the sand. Several workers went ahead of the sleds, pouring water on the sand so that the sleds would slide more easily with their heavy loads.

Around 2500 BCE, King Sneferu tried to build the world's first "true" pyramid with a pointed top and smooth sides. However, his architects did not get the foundation right, and the pyramid collapsed before it was finished, killing hundreds of workers. Sneferu tried again. His architects designed a better foundation, but they built the second pyramid at a 55-degree angle. It was too steep, making it unstable, so the architects adjusted the angle to 43 degrees about halfway up. The pyramid did not fall, but it looked distorted, as if it were bent. His architects tried again, successfully building the entire third pyramid at a 43-degree angle.

The Bent Pyramid, Sneferu's second attempt [14]

The next pharaoh was Khufu, most likely Sneferu's son. He built the world's highest pyramid. At about 481 feet high, the Great Pyramid was the world's tallest building for nearly four thousand years until the Lincoln Cathedral was built in England. The only way for Egypt to achieve such a stunning feat was by having a strong central government. The Egyptians considered their pharaohs divine kings, intermediaries between heaven and earth. Thus, they allowed their kings to wield absolute power.

How did the Egyptians build their pyramids so well that most are still standing over four millennia later? For the Great Pyramid, they had to move 2.3 million stone blocks, each weighing about 2.5 tons. How did they pull off this massive feat without the wheel, cranes, and pulleys? How did they lift those blocks to the height of a forty-eight-story skyscraper?

NOVA's 1992 film, *This Old Pyramid*,[4] used a crew to replicate how they thought the Egyptians did it. They discovered that twelve men could cut 186 stones by hand in a quarry in three weeks; however, they cheated a bit and used iron tools and a winch. To build the Great Pyramid in twenty years, the builders needed 340 stones a day. The researchers estimated that with more primitive tools, it would take 1,200 men to carve 340 stones each day and get the 2.5-ton blocks to the surface.

Fortunately, stone quarries were located where the Egyptians built the pyramids at Giza. They did not have to transport the core stones of the pyramids from elsewhere. Nevertheless, it would take about twelve men to drag each stone on a sled over wet sand from the quarry to the pyramid construction site. If each team could transport two blocks a day, it would require approximately 2,000 men to move 340 massive stones to the building site each day.

Pyramids at Giza [5]

Once the gargantuan blocks arrived at the construction site, men cut each rock into the perfect shape to fit on the pyramid wall. The stone sat on a cobble with levers, allowing two workers to pivot it as two to four men carved. After that, another team of workers pushed the enormous stones up temporary ramps that ran from the ground to the top level of the pyramid. Once they completed the core, they finished the exterior of the pyramid with polished white limestone.

---

[4] "This Old Pyramid" Transcript, *NOVA*, PBS Airdate: February 4, 1997. https://www.pbs.org/wgbh/nova/transcripts/1915mpyramid.html.

Despite old movies showing the Egyptians with whips in hand, forcing the Israelites to labor on the pyramids, the builders were not the Hebrews, nor were they enslaved people from central Africa. The Great Pyramid was built around 2600 BCE. According to Biblical accounts, Abraham was born in Ur about four centuries later. The Israelites did not exist yet. Native Egyptians built the pyramids, according to an analysis of bones found in the worker cemeteries at Giza. Most likely, the laborers were farmers who worked on the pyramids during the offseason when the Nile overflowed its banks and they could not do any farming.

The Great Sphinx of Giza [16]

Khufu's son Khafre built a pyramid next to the Great Pyramid that seems higher, yet this is an optical illusion. It is on higher ground. Khafre built the Great Sphinx next to his pyramid. The gigantic statue, sixty-six feet high and 240 feet long, had a lion's body and a human head. Over thousands of years, sandstorms buried the Great Sphinx up to its neck in sand. Archaeologists unearthed the rest of it in the 1800s. It was once painted in bright blue, red, and yellow.

The Egyptians built most of the pyramids in the Old Kingdom. In the Middle and New Kingdoms, they erected majestic temples. In Luxor, they built the Karnak Temple Complex to Amun-Ra, god of creation. Over twenty shrines graced the Karnak Temple Complex, one of the world's largest worship areas. The central focus was the open-air Hypostyle Hall, with columns sixty-nine feet high. The Avenue of the Sphinxes had six hundred sphinxes lining the path from the Karnak temple to the Luxor temple, almost two miles away.

Hypostyle Hall pillars in the Karnak Temple Complex [17]

The Abu Simbel twin temples are on Lake Nassar's shores, near Egypt's modern-day border with Sudan (known as Nubia when the temples were built). The Egyptians carved the temples out of the mountainside in Rameses II's reign (New Kingdom), completing them in 1265 BCE. Four sixty-six feet high colossal statues of Rameses flank the entrance, two on each side. At the feet of these statues are smaller images of his mother, Mut-Tuy; his chief wife, Nefertari; and his eight oldest children.

Religion permeated every aspect of Egyptian life. Some gods were regional, so when Egypt united, certain gods with similar roles blended together. For instance, the supreme god Amun (Atum) was the creator, but so was Ra, the sun god. Sometimes, he was called Amun-Ra. In Egyptian mythology, before creation, the chaotic ocean of Nun existed in a state of darkness. In one version of the creation myth, a primeval goose called the Great Cackler laid an egg. Amun-Ra hatched from the egg as the sun. Amun pulled an island out of the water and spat, creating Shu, the god of the air. Next, he vomited and created Tefnut, the rain goddess. Shu and Tefnut conceived Nut, the sky goddess, and Geb, the earth god.

Tefnut, the rain goddess and mother of earth and sky [18]

The Egyptians believed that when the world was created, it was an orderly place with plenty of everything that anyone needed. However, the people rebelled against Ra, disrupting the cosmic order and bringing suffering to the world. The primary duty of the pharaoh and his people was to restore "Maat," or the cosmic order. They had to live in harmony with each other and with the gods. Their fate in the afterlife was determined by the balance and harmony they sustained while living.

The Egyptians believed that when they died, the black jackal god Anubis waited for them with his scale at the gates of the underworld. Anubis put the person's heart on one side of the scale and a feather on the other. Were their hearts as light as a feather? If the person had lived in peace and harmony, their heart would be light enough for them to enter Duat, the underworld. Ammit, the crocodile-headed goddess, ate people with heavy hearts who had been disruptive and argumentative in their lifetimes.

Ammit waits (center right) as Anubis (center left) weighs a heart. [19]

Why did the ancient Egyptians mummify their dead? They believed the body had to be preserved for the soul to continue living. The god Anubis also presided over this process.

First, the priests cut out the body's organs and put them in jars of natron salt to dry out. They covered the body with natron salt for seventy days, then applied black resin, which prevented fungal growth. The organs were returned to the body or placed in jars and buried with the body. The priests wrapped the body with linen strips before burial. The priests placed a mask, painted to resemble the person, over the linen-wrapped face and placed the body in a wooden coffin. If the dead person had been wealthy or powerful, they lowered the coffin into a stone sarcophagus with the person's image painted on it. The Egyptians understood the science of mummification so well that some mummies have survived in remarkably good condition to the present day.

The Egyptians also possessed exceptional knowledge in fields such as mathematics and medicine. The Ebers Papyrus, written around 1550 BCE, was an ancient medical guide. It featured magic spells, as Egyptians attributed ailments like migraines to evil spirits known as "demon crocodiles." However, the guide also had instructions for contraception, treating burns, and setting broken bones. The Egyptian doctors would take a person's pulse to check for a firm heartbeat and rule out blockage. The guide discussed diabetes, cancer, and dementia.

While the Sumerians and other Mesopotamian cultures were writing on clay tablets, the Egyptians developed sheets of paper-like papyrus by 2550 BCE. It was made from the pith of the papyrus reeds that grew in the water. The Egyptians developed a 365-day calendar by 3000 BCE, with three distinct seasons: the Nile flooding, winter, and harvest. They tracked the height of the Nile each year during the flood season by marking a column or measuring how high the water came up steps leading down to the river.

With limited cloud cover, the ancient Egyptians were stargazers with an exceptional understanding of astronomy. They knew the difference between stars and planets by the way planets moved through the sky. In the Old Kingdom, the Egyptians aligned their pyramids with the pole star Thuban, also known as "the Serpent," in the Draco constellation. Thuban was almost precisely due north five thousand years ago.

Ancient Egypt's rich culture and scientific understanding have left an enduring legacy that has spanned the ages.

# Chapter 3: The Indus Valley

The Indus Valley Civilization, one of the world's most enigmatic cultures, was at its apex from around 2600 to 1900 BCE. It had a population of up to five million people in the villages and cities that clustered along the Indus River in present-day Pakistan, India, and Afghanistan. Its cities of Harappa and Mohenjo-daro were remarkably advanced in urban planning, architecture, and societal organization. What were the Indus Valley Civilization's sophisticated achievements? They included standardized weights and measures, elaborate drainage systems, and a yet-to-be deciphered script.

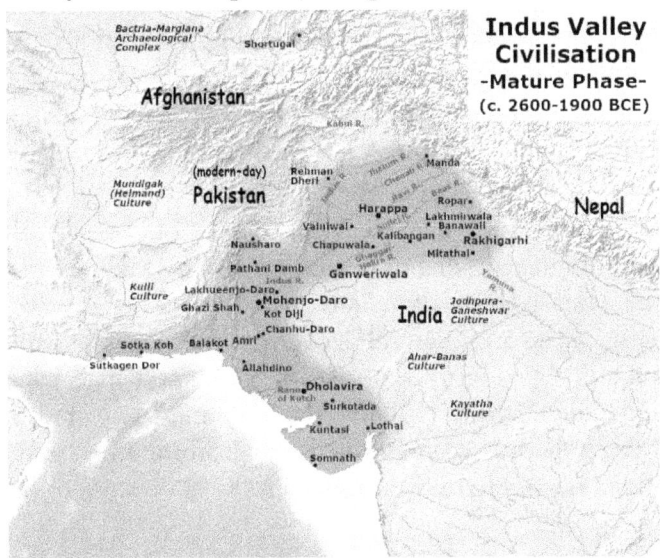

Map of the Indus Valley Civilization [90]

Several years after the British East India Company annexed the Punjab region of northwest India in 1849, they were building a railway near the village of Harappa. The builders found mounds and even partial walls of fire-baked bricks. The more the British workers dug, the more bricks they found—hundreds of thousands.

"They have always been there," the locals told them. "Sometimes we use those bricks when we need to build something."

Archaeologist James Lewis (pseudonym Charles Masson) had explored the area several decades earlier and reported on the ancient artifacts he discovered. Unaware, or uncaring, the British workers dug up the four-thousand-year-old bricks to build the track ballast for the railway line.

In the early 1900s, John Marshall, the new leader of the Archaeological Survey of India, ordered the excavation of Harappa's site. Marshall had just learned of Mohenjo-daro (Mound of the Dead), four hundred miles south of Harappa in today's Pakistan, where similar bricks and artifacts had been found, along with human bones. Both sites represented an ancient and previously unknown civilization that emerged around 3300 BCE. These discoveries revised notions of when advanced civilization originated in the Indian subcontinent.

Since that time, around one thousand sites have been uncovered, including five cities with populations of twenty to forty thousand, or even higher. The ancient people did not build these towns and cities haphazardly. They employed urban planning, meticulously following a grid pattern. Covered drains running throughout Mohenjo-daro were among the world's first sanitation systems. The cities had public baths, irrigation canals, and brick houses with multiple stories. Bricks were a standard size, and so was the width of the roads.

Curiously, the Indus Valley Civilization did not appear to have grand palaces, monuments, or elaborate tombs for its kings. Did they even have kings? The sophistication and urban planning involved in their cities suggest a strong central government. Perhaps they had a government run by a group of people, like a tribal confederation. However, a statuette from Mohenjo-daro, dating to around 2000 BCE, depicts an elegantly dressed man with neatly trimmed hair and beard and a ribbon on his head. He may have been a priest or king (or both).

A seven-inch image of a man from Mohenjo-daro [21]

Another thing missing was temples, which were abundant in ancient Mesopotamia and Egypt, as well as in India in later years. Some historians think the Indus Valley Civilization had no organized religion. However, that is not necessarily the case. The ancient Indo-Iranian religion was a precursor to the Vedic religion, which emerged in northwest India around 1500 BCE (and eventually gave birth to Hinduism). The Indo-Iranian and Vedic religions had few cult images (idols). Typically, worship took place in the open air. The rare temples were simple affairs where a sacred fire burned perpetually. Although the Indus Valley Civilization had no temples or idols, its artwork displayed mythical animals and apparent deities.

Where did the people of the Indus Valley Civilization come from? In a mountainous region of Pakistan, west of the Indus River, a Neolithic people settled Mehrgarh by 5500 BCE and possibly as early as 7000 BCE. Mehrgarh flourished concurrently with the Ubaid, Hassuna, and Samarra cultures in Mesopotamia. Like these cultures, the people of Mehrgarh were nomadic herders of sheep, goats, and cattle who eventually settled down to grow wheat and barley. Some scholars think they migrated to Pakistan from Mesopotamia.

Like the Ubaid and early Egyptians, the people of Mehrgarh had brilliant blue lapis lazuli ornaments by 5500 BCE, which meant they were trading with ancient Afghanistan, a nearby source of the precious stone. Archaeologists have discovered evidence that the Mehrgarh people had basic knowledge of dentistry. They found eleven molars that had been drilled, apparently because of decay. Evidently, the ancient "dentists" used bow drills, which were generally used for friction to create fire or bore holes into wood.

Historians divide the Indus Valley Civilization's history into three phases: Early Harappan (3300-2600 BCE), Mature Harappan (2600-1900 BCE), and Late Harappan (1900-1500 BCE). Among its earliest settlements was Kot Diji in today's Sindh province of Pakistan. Kot Diji was established around 3300 BCE across the Indus River from where Mohenjo-daro was later built. A fertile flood plain surrounded the town, which meant lush farmland and grassland for herds. Fish and wild game were plentiful.

In the Early Harappan era, the people built their houses from sun-dried mud bricks on stone foundations. They made pottery using a potter's wheel. Archaeologists got excited when they dug up a toy cart at Kot Diji from this era. The Indus Valley people were using the transportation wheel by 2600 BCE.

The Great Bath of Mohenjo-daro with a domed granary in the back [22]

The Mature Harappan period was a time when vast cities were built following a master plan with flat-roofed, multiple-story brick houses. By this time, the Indus Valley people worked with copper, bronze, and gold, but not iron (which did not begin for another millennium). They grew cotton and wove it into clothing. Each city had its own administration, but no central government united the cities.

Like the ancient Ubaid and Egyptian civilizations, the people of the Indus Valley Civilization used small, rectangular stone stamp seals to "sign" their names by 2600 BCE. The picture on a seal was usually an animal, like an elephant, rhinoceros, or tiger, with an inscription carved above it. The Indus Valley people passed a cord through a hole in the seal and wore it hanging from their necks.

Intriguingly, carvings of long-necked male unicorns appeared on tablets and over half the stamp seals from 2600 to 1900 BCE in Harappa and Mohenjo-daro. The unicorn always faces a fire-altar, like the ones that burned perpetually in Indo-Iranian and Vedic worship. The one-horned creature must have held a significant religious meaning. Carvings often showed him with stripes on his head and chest but not on the back part of his body.

A stamp seal depicting a unicorn with a fire altar under his chin, circa 2200 BCE. He may represent the god Vishnu. The script at the top of the seal has not been deciphered, but it shows three apparent fish emblems.[28]

Could he have been a two-horned animal, but his other horn did not show up in his profile? Stamp seals with hump-backed bulls and other two-horned creatures showed both horns, even in profile. Archaeologist John Marshall suggested a connection between the unicorn and the Vedic sun-god Vishnu. Another name for Vishnu was "Ekasringa," which referred to a single-horned creature that may have been a rhinoceros or a unicorn.

Unicorns sometimes appear in Bronze-Age Iranian and Mesopotamian art, looking more like a cow or antelope than a horse. Were they real animals? No one has found skeletal remains. However, the ancient Greeks said they lived in India. Ctesias, a Greek doctor who served in Persia's royal court around 405–358 BCE, said a unicorn was a type of wild ass with a twenty-eight-inch horn and a red, white, or black coat.

One Harappan stamp seal shows a tiger with feathery horns fending off an attack by a faun-like female creature. She has ox-like horns and a female body above the waist. Below her waist, she has the body and long tail of an animal. Some scholars think the bottom half is a tiger, but it has no stripes. Her tail is also thick, unlike the elegant tail of the tiger in front of her, and she appears to have cleft feet. Whether she is a goddess or a mythical figure is unclear.

Stamp seal with a faun-like female attacking a horned tiger [44]

The people of the Indus Valley Civilization traded with southern Mesopotamia. They adopted the stamp seal from the Sumerians but not the cylinder seal. They also adopted a common motif of Gilgamesh fighting wild cats, as told in the *Epic of Gilgamesh*. In the Mesopotamian version, Gilgamesh fights two lions, but in the Indus Valley version, he fights two tigers. Did the Indus Valley people know the Gilgamesh story, or were they simply copying the motif? Hopefully, a bright person will one day decode the Harappan script and reveal the civilization's mysteries.

Indus Valley "Gilgamesh" fights two tigers. Note the script at the top.[35]

Mohenjo-daro had the "Great Bath" in the Mature Harappan period. The pool was thirty-nine feet long, twenty-three feet wide, and almost eight feet deep. It was the world's first public water tank. Steps led down into the pool. A ledge above the water led from the stairs to the other end of the pool. People could walk along it without getting into the water. The floor and walls of the Great Bath were made from tightly fitted bricks held together with gypsum plaster and covered with bitumen.

A row of brick columns lined the pool on three sides, and two massive doors were at the south end. One room on the eastern side of the pool had a well to supply water. Rainwater may have also provided the pool with water. What was the purpose of the Great Bath? Was it a place for recreation? Some scholars think it was for religious purification, something like the practice of modern Hindus who bathe in the Ganges River to cleanse their souls from sin, cure illnesses, and connect with the divine.

Each neighborhood in the Indus Valley cities had a public well. Mohenjo-daro had over seven hundred public wells, and many homes had private wells. Saqiyahs and shadoofs brought the water up from underground. A shadoof uses a pole with a bucket and a counterweight. A saqiyah, still used in India, resembles a water wheel but features both a horizontal wheel and a vertical wheel. An ox or donkey turns the horizontal wheel, which has a drive shaft connected to the vertical wheel. As the vertical wheel turns, buckets on the wheel scoop up the water.

A "Punjab" or saqiyah wheel in India, 1917 [16]

In the cities, houses had a courtyard with a toilet hole. The waste was "flushed" with a bucket of water into an underground clay brick pipe that led to a brick drain that ran along the street. They also had rooftop toilets with terracotta pipes leading to the street drain. Sewage drained into a "soak pit" or cesspit. Occasionally, workers scooped out the solid waste to fertilize the fields. Liquid waste soaked into the ground. Drains running along the streets had holes leading to the street for clearing blockages.

The city of Dholavira had a sophisticated system of water storage featuring stone channels and tanks, which were among the earliest in the world. Dholavira was semi-arid and prone to droughts, so if the people could store the water from the monsoons, they could survive. At least sixteen massive reservoirs captured rainwater during the monsoon season, as well as from two streams that flowed during the rainy season but dried up for the rest of the year. The city had a rectangular step-well that was larger than the Great Bath in Mohenjo-daro.

The people of the Indus Valley Civilization had extraordinary technological skills. They made most of their pottery by throwing it on a potter's wheel, which leaves characteristic rings on the inside of the pot. They heated lime to use it as plaster. They used furnaces to bake bricks and fire pottery. With exceptional skill, they cut, drilled, and polished beads, which they made from a variety of stones like agate, carnelian, jasper, lapis lazuli, and steatite. With alkaline etching, they created intricate designs on the beads. The Indus Valley Civilization traded its beads, pottery, and other goods with Mesopotamia, Afghanistan, and Persia. They traveled by boat up the rivers and the Persian Gulf.

The Indus Valley Civilization began writing by at least 2800 BCE. Centuries earlier, pictographs appeared on pottery and other materials. About two thousand unearthed stamp seals have a script on them. Archaeologists also discovered inscriptions on pottery, weapons, tools, and copper plates. Altogether, about five thousand examples of the Harappan, or ancient Indus Valley, script have been found. Frustratingly, no one has unlocked its meaning. This keeps us from fully understanding the language, religion, and administrative systems of these fascinating people.

The Harappan script has between four hundred and seven hundred signs; however, only sixty-seven were used regularly. Some are seemingly obvious, such as a fish sign. However, multiple variations of a fish-like sign appear in the same row of script. Some scholars suggest a connection between the Harappan script and the Proto-Elamite script used in southwestern Iran at the same time as the Indus Valley Civilization. The Proto-Elamite script has not been translated either, but thirty-five signs are similar to the Harappan script. Proto-Elamite also has signs in common with Mesopotamian cuneiform, especially the number system.

Some archaeologists argue that the Indus Valley Civilization did not have a military. They say that the defensive walls were for flood control, not to repel invading armies. The Indus Valley Civilization had knives, spears, bows, and arrows, but these tools could have been for hunting. They had figurines and stamp seals of dancers and animals, but no artwork showing warriors. However, evidence indicates that the Indus Valley was far from a peaceful utopia. Skeletal remains of males show high rates of injury, especially to the face and skull, characteristic of battle wounds.

Some people at Harappa had leprosy and tuberculosis. They were buried outside the southeastern part of Harappa. Oddly, the men with fatal head wounds were buried at the same site. Could the men who died of head injuries have been executed or sacrificed? Were they bludgeoned to death? Otherwise, why bury the warriors with the lepers? The number of crushed skulls and victims of leprosy and tuberculosis increased toward the end of the Mature Harappan period and into its decline in the Late Harappan period. Did disease and violence close the chapter on the Indus Valley Civilization?

Climate change also played a role, as rainfall decreased and the deserts expanded. Tectonic activity was at play in that era. The large, moving plates of Earth's crust created uplift and probable earthquakes along the Makran coast, leaving coastal cities miles inland. Rivers shifted and even dried up, disrupting the robust trade on the waterways. Meanwhile, Indo-Aryan people from the Central Asian steppes were migrating in, vying for resources. The Indus Valley Civilization declined to such an extent that its people lost their knowledge of writing and hydraulic engineering. The culture had nearly disappeared by 1500 BCE.

# Chapter 4: The Mysteries of the Minoans and Mycenaeans

The legendary Minoans and Mycenaeans flourished in the Bronze Age. The Minoans' sophisticated society centered on the large island of Crete, which lies in the Mediterranean Sea between North Africa and Greece's mainland. They had impressive palaces, intricate art, and extensive trade networks. As the Minoan civilization declined, the Mycenaeans developed a magnificent civilization on the Greek mainland and Crete, incorporating aspects of Minoan culture. The Mycenaeans were the immortalized heroes of Homer's *Iliad* and *Odyssey*.

The Minoans emerged from a Neolithic culture on the island of Crete around 3500 BCE. Where did the name "Minoan" come from? Greek mythology says Minos was the first king of Crete. His father was the god Zeus, and his mother was a Phoenician princess from Lebanon whom Zeus kidnapped.

About 2000 BCE, the culture suddenly became more complex, and the Minoans began building cities and palaces. This likely happened in King Minos's reign. (He was probably a real person around whom myths evolved.) Thucydides, a fifth-century BCE Greek historian, said King Minos built the first navy. The Minoans controlled the eastern Mediterranean trade, and their pottery has been found on the Iberian Peninsula (Spain and Portugal).

Just as the Minoans were starting their great leap forward, the palaces they built came crashing down. Crete had consequential seismic activity between 2000 and 1700 BCE. The island is located where the African and Eurasian tectonic plates meet and is one of the most earthquake-prone places in Europe.

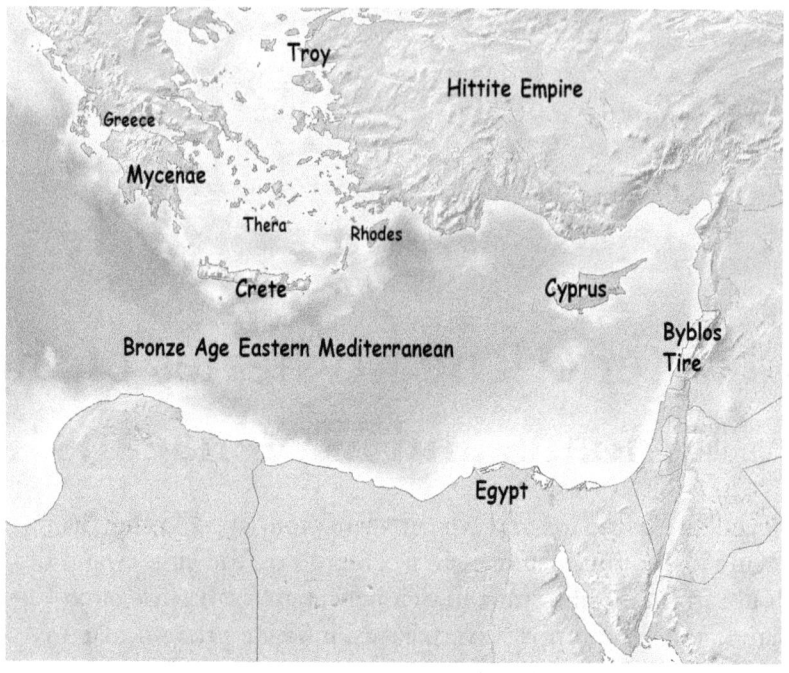

Crete's strategic location [27]

Nevertheless, the resilient Minoans rebuilt their palaces on a grander scale, showcasing advanced architecture and engineering. The palace at Knossos was four stories high, with massive colonnades. It had nearly a thousand rooms and covered an area larger than two football fields. Spectacular frescoes in bold colors decorated the walls.

The palaces served as hubs for industry, trade, and administration. Stockpiles of oil, grain, and wine were stored in the palaces, likely intended for trade or as emergency stores in the event of a famine. Workshops produced ceramics and exquisite figurines that were traded around the Mediterranean and Aegean seas.

At first, the cities on Crete were independent realms. After the Minoans rebuilt the collapsed palaces around 1700 BCE, Knossos ruled over the other cities on the island. By this time, Knossos and its nearby villages had about 100,000 people. Crete had roads connecting the major cities to each other and to the surrounding farms and villages. The Minoan civilization reached its peak between 1650 and 1450 BCE.

The Minoans possessed a sophisticated understanding of hydraulics. Aqueducts brought water to the cities and towns. Some were simple affairs, such as open ditches traveling downhill from the mountains. Others were closed, terracotta pipes. The palace at Knossos had a ten-mile aqueduct supplying water from mountain springs. The Minoans also had sewage systems for their cities, using clay pipes.

This palace at Knossos has been partially restored and painted.[28]

Crete's palaces housed libraries of clay tablets inscribed with Cretan hieroglyphs and the Linear A script. Minoans began using Cretan hieroglyphics, Europe's first written language, around 2100 BCE. No one has yet decoded this language, but its pictographs on clay tablets and stamp seals bear slight similarities to Egyptian hieroglyphics. However, Cretan hieroglyphics had only eighty-five symbols, compared to Egypt's eight hundred. This means the Cretan written language was phonetic, with the symbols standing for sounds.

Around 1800 BCE, the Minoans began using a new writing system, Linear A. They used both scripts for about a century, then abandoned the Cretan hieroglyphics. Linear A was also phonetic, with a simpler script, and more like a true alphabet. It may have been influenced by the Proto-Sinaitic script, which evolved into the Phoenician alphabet. Linear A has letters in common with the Phoenician alphabet, like the symbol that looks like our *Y* but stood for the *W* sound. Another shared symbol was a circle with a cross inside, which stood for the *T* sound in Phoenician. Scholars have been able to decipher the phonetic sounds of the Linear A symbols; however, they remain uncertain about the language that Linear A represents.

**A tablet with Linear A written on it**[29]

Several ancient sources say that the Minoans expanded their territory by conquering other lands. They settled the islands of Kythera, Melos, Rhodes, and Thera in the Aegean Sea. According to Thucydides, Minos annexed the Cyclades islands that lie north of Crete between Greece and Anatolia (Turkey). He also said that Minos attacked Athens, which was a small settlement at the time. The biblical book of Deuteronomy states that the Minoans (also known as the Caphtorites) invaded Gaza, destroyed the Avvites who lived there, and settled in their place (Deuteronomy 2:23). According to biblical chronology, this occurred before 1400 BCE.

Minoan ceramics were highly sought after as trade items. The Minoans crafted cups with handles that resemble today's teacups and coffee mugs. Their figurines showed men wearing loincloths and a bare-breasted goddess with a long, tiered skirt grasping a snake in each hand. The Minoans decorated their pottery with bold, black swirls and other geometric designs. They also featured images of dolphins, fish, octopi, ibexes, and flowers.

A Minoan octopus jug from Zakros, Crete, circa 1600-1450 BCE.[80]

The Minoans' striking artwork offers a glimpse into their culture, religion, and aesthetic sensibilities. The Hagia Triada sarcophagus, circa 1400 BCE, was crafted from limestone and adorned with frescoes. It depicts priests and priestesses making offerings and sacrificing bulls. Bulls were not the only sacrifice. Archaeologists have found grim evidence of child sacrifice and cannibalism. In one case, an earthquake struck, burying the priests and their sacrificial victim, an adolescent boy, under tons of rubble.

The Minoans even had a bull-vaulting ceremony. A man would take a bull by the horns and somersault over its back.

Perhaps the importance of the bull alluded to the ancient myth of Minos. The sea god Poseidon gifted Minos with a resplendent, pure white bull to underscore Minos's divine right to rule. Minos was supposed to sacrifice the bull to Poseidon, but he was so taken with the bull that he kept it and sacrificed another bull instead. Poseidon got his revenge by causing the king's wife to fall in love with the bull, which impregnated her. The baby was a hideous Minotaur, a half-bull, half-man monster who ate people. Minos kept the creature in a labyrinth but had to feed it humans. After conquering Athens, he made the people send him seven boys and seven girls as food for the Minotaur every nine years. The Athenians sent the children twice, but the third time, the semi-divine hero Theseus accompanied the youngsters and killed the monster.

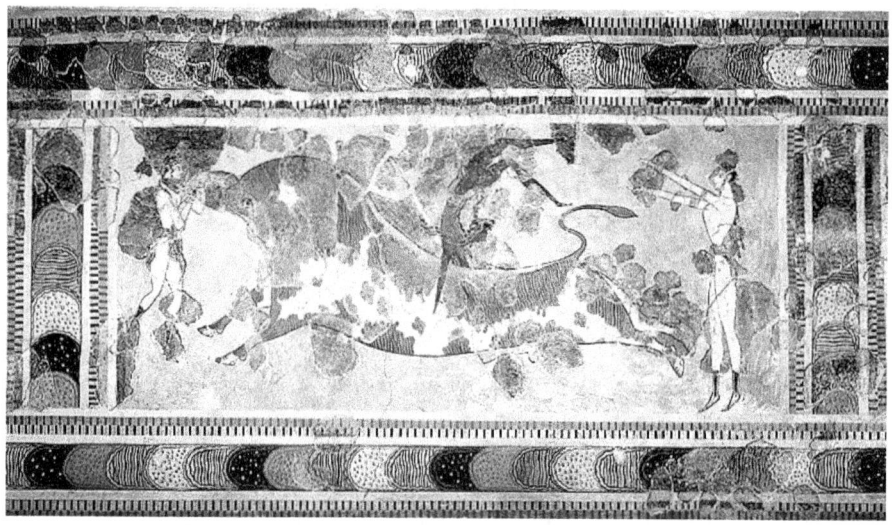

This fresco from Knossos shows a man flipping over a bull. [81]

Around 1600 BCE, a horrific volcanic eruption with a VEI-7 magnitude destroyed the island of Thera, about 120 miles north of Crete. Ten million tons of ash and rock shot up twenty miles, then buried all life on Thera. The eruption triggered earthquakes and a devastating tsunami that buried the northern part of Crete under water. Cities and ports were gone in minutes. The Minoans in southern Crete survived and struggled on in a weakened state. Losing over half its ships and ports devastated Crete's trade-based economy.

To the south, the Mycenaeans of Greece's mainland were rising in strength. They snatched up the Minoans' former sea trade and established colonies around the Aegean and eastern Mediterranean. About 1450 BCE, the Mycenaeans launched an attack on Crete, torching its palaces and temples. Although they destroyed much of Knossos, they spared its palace and renovated it for their own use. The Minoans and Mycenaeans lived together on Crete for several centuries, but the Mycenaeans became the ruling class. Crete switched from using Linear A to the Mycenaeans' Linear B script.

People had lived on the mainland of Greece since the Neolithic Age, and one early area of civilization was on the Peloponnese Peninsula. During the Neolithic Age, people in this area constructed their houses using stone blocks and cultivated crops on terraces rising up the hills. In the early Bronze Age, they built at least two coastal cities that are now submerged because of rising sea levels and earthquakes.

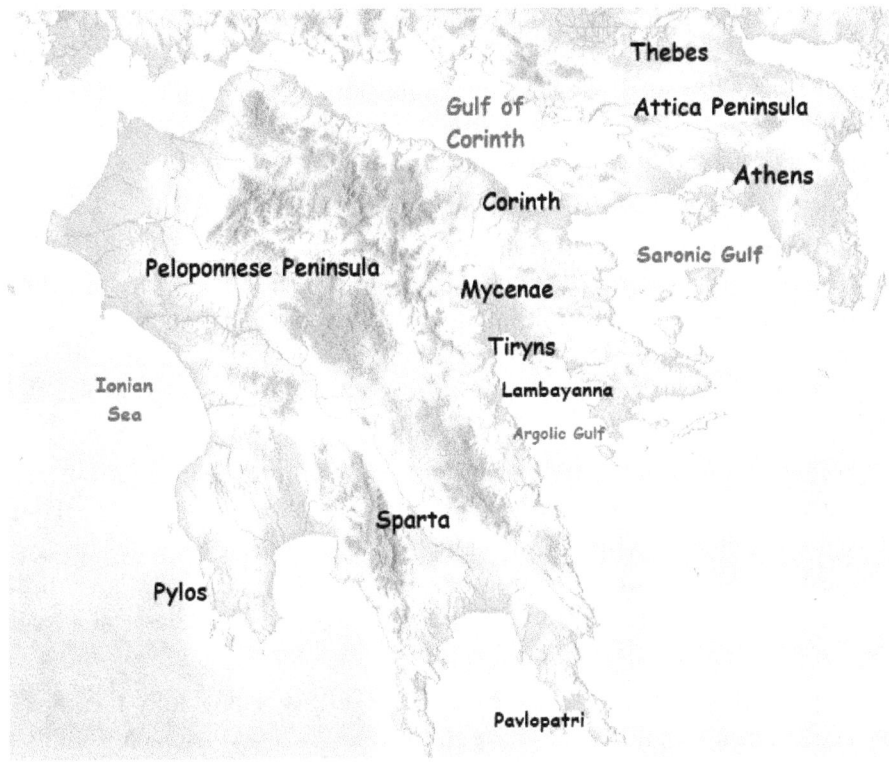

Southern Greece in the Mycenaean Civilization [83]

The Greek philosopher Plato wrote of the lost city of Atlantis, an advanced society that sank into the ocean as punishment for moral decay. Perhaps one of these cities gave rise to the legend. The cities had colossal foundations, fortified walls, two-story houses, temples, tombs, water pipes, paved roads, and towers. One sunken city is Pavlopetri, which had a population of up to two thousand people just off the island of Elafonisos. The other is Lambayanna, in the Bay of Kiladhaom.

Did the Mycenaeans build these seaside cities? It is unlikely. The Mycenaean civilization emerged around 1750 BCE, and these two cities were built approximately a thousand years before that. The Minoans were present, but they had not yet built complex cities. An earlier civilization, perhaps a precursor to the Minoans and Mycenaeans, built these cities.

However, Pavlopetri did not sink until around 1100 BCE, so it lasted through the Minoan and Mycenaean cultures. Artifacts show that the Minoans traded with Pavlopetri and that the Mycenaeans lived there. The Mycenaeans were masterful assimilators, borrowing from Minoan culture and whoever built the underwater cities. Yet, these "long-haired Achaeans," as Homer called them, took architecture, engineering, art, and military tactics to the next level.

The Peloponnesian Peninsula positioned the Mycenaeans in a strategic location for sea trade and cultural interaction with other civilizations. They traded in the Black Sea and, like the Minoans, their pottery has been found in Spain. The Mycenaeans exported linen, olives, olive oil, pottery, raisins, wine, and wool textiles. They imported copper from Cyprus, tin from the western Mediterranean (possibly even Britain), and gold and ivory from Egypt.

Highly militant, the Mycenaeans not only conquered Crete but also triumphed over southern Greece, including ancient Athens. Their brilliant engineers achieved seemingly impossible feats with bridges, defensive walls, and wastewater systems. The exploits of these overachievers were so legendary that they lived on in Classical Greek lore.

Tiryns, which overlooked the Argolic Gulf, was probably the oldest Mycenaean city, dating to the Neolithic Age. The Mycenaeans built a fortress there about 1600 BCE. By 1300 BCE, it had become a chief port with a population of approximately ten thousand people. Colossal "Cyclopean" walls surrounded Tiryns, and within these walls was a labyrinth of vaulted tunnels. What was the purpose of the tunnels? They may have been storage areas or secret hiding places if invaders overcame the city. The Mycenaeans built a palace in Tiryns around 1400 BCE; however, an earthquake collapsed it about two centuries later. Although they did not rebuild the palace, Tiryns continued to thrive. It even survived Greece's Dark Ages, a time when most cities crumpled.

Two lions guard the top of the colossal gate of Mycenae. [88]

Mycenae, north of the Saronic Gulf, was the hub of the Mycenaean civilization. It had a population of thirty thousand at its peak. This city on a cliff in the Peloponnese Peninsula had defensive walls over eighteen feet thick. With mind-blowing engineering, the Mycenaeans used enormous twenty-ton limestone boulders in the wall. The largest stones weighed over one hundred tons.

Part of the walls and the gate still stand today, after three millennia. No wonder the Greeks believed that mythical creatures like the Cyclops built the walls! How could ordinary humans lift a hundred-ton rock? However, the Mycenaeans likely used ramps and a system of rollers. Mycenae's Lion Gate, built about 1250 BCE, had a twenty-ton lintel supported by ten-foot-high boulders. Two lions stand on the lintel, hence the name.

Intriguingly, Hattusa, the capital of the Hittite Empire, also had colossal walls and a lion gate eerily similar to Mycenae's. The Hittites built their lion gate first, about a century before the one in Greece. Although the Mycenaeans may have interacted with the Hittites through trade, Hattusa was in the center of today's Turkey, nowhere near a coast. Yet, somehow, the Greeks learned of the gate and copied it.

The gate raises another question: why lions? Did Greece have lions? Yes, lions lived in the Peloponnese Peninsula until around 1000 BCE. Lions frequently appeared in Mycenaean art, usually in hunting scenes, symbolizing power and authority.

Mycenaeans typically built their cities around a hill—a custom that the Greeks continued in the Archaic and Classical periods. They built towering walls to fortify the hill, called an acropolis. This is where the Mycenaeans built their palaces and temples. The rest of the city surrounded the acropolis. Guardsmen posted on the hill could scan the surrounding terrain for hostile forces. If enemies attacked the city, the citizens dashed inside the acropolis for safety. The soldiers on the acropolis had the uphill advantage for shooting arrows and other missiles at the attackers.

Each of the major cities ruled a state that had smaller towns. Every state had an *anax*, or king, who governed that region and its industries. He was also the region's judge and commander-in-chief of the regional army. All the kings answered to a "great king," whose capital was probably Mycenae. He had a council of elders who advised him, a tradition that continued in later Greek periods.

The Mycenaeans had a hierarchical society. At the top were the king and the warrior aristocracy. The Mycenaeans buried their royals and aristocrats in "tholos" tombs, which were immense beehive structures with domes and decorative corbels built into hillsides. At the bottom of the Mycenaean society were captured people, enslaved to work in the temples and palaces. Some enslaved people could own land. Most people in Mycenaean society fell into the middle class—the craftspeople, farmers, and merchants.

The Mycenaeans adapted the Linear A script used by the Minoans into a new script known as Linear B. It used similar symbols as Linear A but added some new ones. Linear B, which has been translated, represented an ancient form of Greek that the Mycenaeans spoke. No one knows what language the Minoans spoke.

The tablet on the left and the drawing of it on the right have a list of women's names.⁴⁴

In 1932 CE, a fourteen-year-old boy in England, Michael Ventris, attended a lecture by archaeologist Sir Arthur Evans on the Linear B script. No one had decoded it. His interest piqued. In his twenties, Ventris attempted to unlock the language through statistical analysis. He realized it was an archaic Greek dialect. Partnering with Cambridge linguist John Chadwick, he cracked the code of Linear B. Sadly, Ventris died in an automobile accident before publishing their findings. Once scholars could read the script, they realized that written Linear B was a language of record-keeping and administrative affairs. Greek literature did not emerge in written form until Homer and Hesiod began writing epic poetry after the Greek Dark Ages.

However, even record-keeping opened a window on Mycenaean culture. Lists of sacrifices offered to the gods, like spices and honey, revealed that the Mycenaeans worshipped many of the same deities as in the Archaic and Classical Greek eras that followed. The chief Mycenaean god was Poseidon, the sea deity, whom they called "Po-se-da-o." Other gods included Zeus, Dionysus, Hera, Ares, and Artemis.

Mycenaean women worshippers in a mural from the palace of Thebes[86]

Homer wrote in the *Iliad* that the Mycenaean "Great King" Agamemnon led one thousand Greek ships across the Aegean Sea to invade Troy. The Trojan prince Paris had stolen Helen, wife of King Menelaus of Sparta, who was Agamemnon's brother. Yet, the Trojan War had a practical reason. Troy (in northwestern Turkey) was strategically located on the Dardanelles Strait, linking the Aegean and Black Seas. Whoever controlled the Dardanelles controlled the lucrative Black Sea trade.

Homer wrote that after a grueling ten-year war, the Mycenaeans emerged victorious (circa 1180 BCE), and King Menelaus reclaimed his wife. Yet, the victory came at a crushing cost. In the *Odyssey,* Homer said that while the Greek kings were away for a decade, their realms destabilized. When Great King Agamemnon returned, his wife and her lover killed him. Many of Greece's mighty warriors died fighting Troy. Farms were neglected, and food was scarce.

Was Troy an actual place? Did the Trojan War really happen? Another name Homer used for Troy was "Wilusa," a city with close connections to the Hittite Empire. Homer said the Hittite name of Prince Paris was Alaksandu. The Hittite records said that Alaksandu and the people of Wilusa fought the "Ahhiyawa," possibly the Mycenaean Greeks.

In the late 1800s CE, several amateur archaeologists excavated a low hill at Hisarlik in northwestern Turkey, which they believed might be the ancient site of Troy. They unearthed nine layers, with each new city built over the older one, dating back to approximately 3000 BCE. The archaeologists bungled things and misidentified an older civilization as being Homer's Troy. Nevertheless, later excavations revealed a layer higher up that showed evidence of a prolonged siege and total destruction around 1200 BCE. Troy probably was the real city of Wilusa, and the Trojan War likely was an actual event.

Both the Mycenaean civilization and the Hittite Empire collapsed in the Bronze Age collapse (1200-900 BCE). Yet, war was not the only factor. Archaeological evidence and written records from Syria, Egypt, and the Hittite Empire reveal other horrors of the era. A mega-drought brought starvation conditions to the Eastern Mediterranean. Greek and Syrian cities fell to earthquakes. Probably displaced by war and natural disasters, the mysterious Sea Peoples raided the coastal cities and shattered the sea trade.

Most Greek cities crumbled, although people continued to live in small communities as herders, farmers, and fishers. The Greeks lost their written language for three centuries, and the stunning civilizations created by the Minoans and Mycenaeans dissolved.

# Chapter 5: Ancient China— From Xia to Zhou

Gong Gong, the water god, was having a bad day. He had fought Zhurong, the fire god, and lost. On his way home, he bumped his head on Mount Buzhou. "Ai ya!" he cried, rubbing his head. Then he looked up in horror as a torrent of water poured down. Mount Buzhou was one of the four pillars supporting the sky. Gong Gong had accidentally released the floodgates of heaven.

As the floodwaters rose, King Yao hurried to his advisors, the Four Mountains. "What should I do? The water is covering the Earth!"

"Appoint your cousin, Gun, as your flood control manager," they answered.

Gun stole a divine soil called "xirang" from the gods. It continuously expanded, so he used the soil to build dams and raise the riverbanks. Despite his best efforts, the flooding continued for nine years. King Yao resigned in shame and appointed Shun as his successor. Finally, Gun's son, Yu the Engineer, diverted the water by building the "Dragon Gate," a canal through the mountains that led to the sea. At the end of his life, King Shun made the hero Yu the next ruler. Yu began the Xia dynasty and ruled for forty-five years.

Mythology shrouds ancient China's earliest dynasty, yet archaeological findings provide tantalizing clues that it existed. This chapter delves into the legendary Xia dynasty, the historically documented Shang dynasty, and the influential Zhou dynasty. How did they establish the cultural, political, and philosophical foundations of Chinese civilization that endured for thousands of years? When did the Chinese start writing and working with bronze? What was the Mandate of Heaven? How did significant philosophies like Confucianism, Taoism, and Legalism shape Chinese thought and actions?

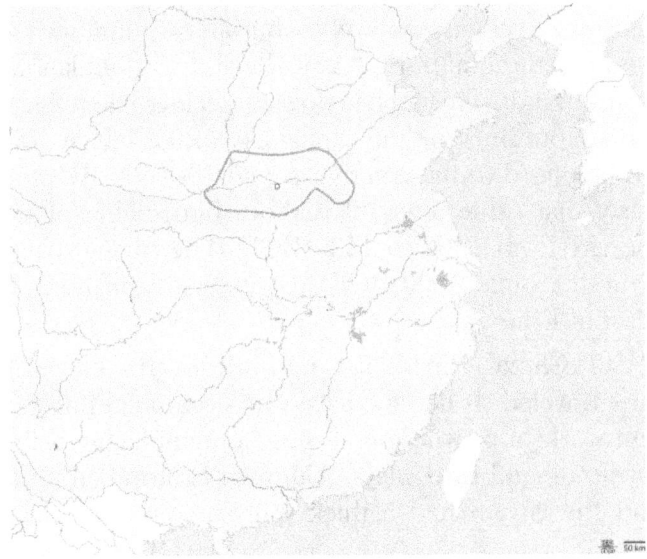

The Xia dynasty's position in China[36]

What records do we have of the Xia, the Shang, and the Zhou dynasties? In the fifth century BCE, Confucius compiled the *Book of Documents* based on earlier works he had collected. It has speeches about the Xia, Shang, and Zhou dynasties receiving the Mandate of Heaven. The *Book of Zhou* (*Zhou Shu*) is a fourth-century BCE collection of histories of the Zhou dynasty. The *Bamboo Annals* begin with Emperor Huangdi (before the Xia Dynasty) and end in 296 BCE, when the *Annals* were buried with King Xiang of Wei in his tomb.

In the early first century BCE, Sima Qian gathered histories from older manuscripts and wrote the *Shiji*, or *Records of the Grand Historian*. It covered China's history, beginning with the legendary Yellow Emperor, who took power around 2697 BCE. Chinese lore says that the Yellow Emperor (Huangdi), an ancestor of Yu the Engineer, invented boats, wheeled carts, the compass, and writing. He also introduced the belief system of Taoism.

Archaeologists have uncovered jade treasures, bronze vessels, and ceramics that they believe date to the Xia era. The problem is that the Chinese were not writing yet, so they left no inscriptions announcing who they were. However, evidence of a prolonged and devastating flooding of the Yellow River supports the legend of a horrendous flood preceding the Xia dynasty.

In 1959 CE, archaeologists unearthed a 745-acre site in the Yiluo Basin of the Yellow River near Luoyang in Henan Province. Its palatial structures, bronze vessels, and elite burials all pointed to a social hierarchy and a central authority. At its height, its population was about twenty-four thousand. The archaeologists decided that the city, which they named Erlitou, must be the capital city of the fabled Xia. Why did they think it belonged to the Xia dynasty (2070–1600 BCE) and not the Shang dynasty that came after it? Radiocarbon dating places the time range of the city from 1860 to 1530 BCE. The Shang dynasty did not take power until around 1600 BCE, and its first capital was Bo, located 191 miles east of Erlitou.

Erlitou had China's first road network over which China's first wheeled carts traveled. It had a palace (or ceremonial hub) at its center, with adjacent workshops where craftspeople manufactured bronze items featuring turquoise and jade inlays. Although Erlitou had no fortification walls around the city, it had a thick wall surrounding the palace and workshops.

The Xia dynasty marked the beginning of China's Bronze Age. At Erlitou, archaeologists found China's first bronze weapons, tools, and ceremonial vessels, including three-legged cups and basins. The city also produced ceramics and bone tools. Its people often buried their family members under or near their houses. In one grave, archaeologists found a dragon sculpture with two thousand pieces of inlaid turquoise and jade.

Bronze dragon with turquoise and jade inlay from Erlitou[87]

Yu the Engineer, the first king of the Xia dynasty, appointed his son, Qi, as the next ruler when he died. This broke precedent. Previously, kings chose their successors based on who they thought would do the best job. The throne did not automatically go to the king's son. Thus, by appointing his son as his successor, Yu began the first Chinese dynasty, a system in which the throne passed from father to son (or to a near relative).

Archaeologists believe that the Wangchenggang archaeological site in Henan Province is Yangcheng, the first capital of the Xia dynasty. The ancient histories say that King Yu built the city near Mount Song on the banks of the Yellow River. He introduced irrigation farming to China and built a powerful military, arming them with bronze crossbows, swords, and spears. The "Xia Calendar" is a lunar calendar that Yu or his descendants developed.

The *Shiji* lists seventeen kings of the Xia dynasty. Few details exist about their lives and reigns because no one wrote about them until centuries later.

The Shang dynasty, like the Xia dynasty, emerged in the Yellow River valley, the cradle of Chinese civilization. It covered the same area as the Xia but expanded east and south until it grew to about three times the size of the Xia dynasty.

At one time, scholars doubted the existence of the Shang dynasty, much as some still doubt the Xia dynasty. Then, the oracle bones showed up with China's earliest writing.

Chinese people have been using medicine allegedly made from dragon bones for thousands of years. In the late 1800s CE, a Chinese scholar named Wang Yirong bought some dragon-bone medicine when he was sick with malaria. Wang and his friend noticed writing scratched on the bones. They went back to the shop and bought all the bones the apothecary had. The "medicine" was not dragon bones but ancient oxen or water buffalo bones. Yet, they were valuable beyond belief, inscribed with ancient writings from thousands of years earlier.

Because the bones are organic material, scholars can carbon date them to within decades of when the animal died. Incredibly, about fifty thousand oracle bones with writing on them have survived until today, despite all the ones that were ground into "dragon-bone" medicine.

Around 1250 BCE, people began carving these inscriptions on bones (usually the shoulder bone of a water buffalo) and turtle shells. At first, they were pictographs. Later, they evolved into the symbols that eventually became Chinese written characters. Priests and fortune tellers used the oracle bones to predict the future. For instance, the king might ask, "If I attack this city, will I win the battle?" The priest wrote his question on one side of a bone. He then turned the bone over and drilled little pits on the back side of the bone. He heated a thin rod until it was red hot, then stuck it into the pits. The heat caused the bone to crack, and the priest interpreted the answer to the question based on how it cracked.

Kings were not the only people who inquired about the future this way. Anyone could consult a fortune teller who used oracle bones.

Chinese scholars have been able to interpret the ancient characters. Although it has evolved over thousands of years, the core principles of written Chinese have remained. Scholars could analyze and interpret the pictographs, ideograms (symbols that represent an idea), and phono-semantic compounds (symbols that represent a sound).

Early Shang dynasty oracle bones with pictographs. The pictographs on the top stone, with a square and a cross under it, mean "child." Today, the character is 子 (zǐ).[38]

Inscriptions from the Shang dynasty have also appeared on bronze ceremonial vessels, pottery, and jade. The people of the era wrote on bamboo and thin pieces of wood, but only a few lasted through the millennia. However, the surviving writing has enabled scholars to confirm the names of kings mentioned in histories written in later dynasties. They provide details about the Shang dynasty's military, administration, and culture.

Replica of a horse-pulled chariot. Horses and chariots came to China during the Shang dynasty.[89]

The Shang dynasty (1600-1046 BCE) began during a thunderstorm when the righteous Cheng Tang, "the perfect," overthrew the tyrannical Xia king, Jie. Cheng Tang's distant ancestor was Xie, who legend says was born after his mother swallowed an egg that a black bird dropped. Xie helped Yu (the first Xia king) control the Great Flood.

For over half a millennium, about thirty kings led the Shang dynasty. The kings also served as high priests, offering sacrifices to their ancestors and Di, the supreme god. Advisors and officials from a hereditary aristocratic class surrounded the king. The dynasty's capital city changed location several times, but Cheng Tang's capital was Shang (near today's Zhengzhou) on the Yellow River in Henan Province, about seventy miles east of Erlitou. Even when later kings chose a different political capital,

Shang persevered as the religious and ceremonial capital, where the ancestral temples remained. Shang's defensive walls were twenty-six feet high and sixty-five feet thick.

The Shang people buried their royal family in massive tombs with jade ornaments, bronze goblets, and oracle bones. They sacrificed people, probably servants, to accompany the royals in the afterlife. The tomb of Fu Hao, a military commander and priestess, was found undisturbed in 1976 CE at Yin, the Shang dynasty's last capital. Archaeologists discovered over seven hundred jade objects, dozens of bronze weapons, battle-axes, six dogs, and sixteen sacrificed humans buried with her. Her husband, King Wu Ding, had sixty-four wives, but she was one of the top three.

The people of the Xia dynasty worked with bronze, but the Shang dynasty's people did piece-mold casting of bronze ceremonial vessels. They made a clay mold with a design and poured molten bronze into it. After it cooled, they cut the clay. Some of the larger bronze pieces weighed two thousand pounds.

A bird-shaped bronze wine container, Zhou dynasty [40]

The last king of the Shang dynasty was Di Xin. He rode out to the Battle of Muve against the rebel King Wu of Zhou, a vassal state. Di Xin's soldiers defected to the Zhou side. When he saw he was in a hopeless situation, Di Xin committed suicide. King Wu made Di Xin's son, Wu Gun, a vassal king under him.

China's longest dynasty (789 years) was the Zhou dynasty (1046-256 BCE). It had two eras, the Western Zhou (1046-771 BCE) and Eastern Zhou (771-256 BCE). The Western Zhou's capital was near today's Xi'an in northern China (Shaanxi Province). A shift in political power forced the court to move over two hundred miles east to Chengzhou, near present-day Luoyang (Henan Province).

Chinese mythology says that the Zhou royalty descended from Qi, who lived during the Xia dynasty. His mother miraculously conceived him when she stepped into the footprint of Shang Di, the supreme god. She thought the strange conception was a bad omen, so she tried to abandon her baby three times. Each time, the child survived with the help of cattle, horses, and birds. Finally, she resolved to keep her baby. After Qi grew up, he taught agriculture to the people; thus, he got the title "Houji" or "Director of Grain" in the Xia dynasty.

Emperor Wu claimed that his authority to attack and conquer the Shang dynasty came from the "Mandate of Heaven." This was the idea that heaven granted the divine right to rule. If an emperor were just and wise, the mandate would remain with him, allowing him to rule for many years. The people considered their emperor the "son of heaven" and were unlikely to challenge his authority. However, if he were unreasonable, tyrannical, or unprincipled, he lost the Mandate of Heaven. Signs that he had lost the mandate included floods, famine, and other natural disasters. If he lost the mandate, people could revolt without fear of heaven's wrath. Revolts from within or invasions from without dethroned the emperor and usually established a new dynasty.

Emperors of the Western Zhou employed a decentralized government model rather than micromanaging everything. Emperor Wu appointed seventy vassal kings, usually loyal friends and family, to govern, keep order, and oversee the resources of each region. Vassal kings had to pay tribute and, if the emperor went to war, they had to provide military personnel. In exchange, the emperor gave his vassals lands and titles. The Western Zhou era became prosperous because of new agricultural methods and advanced metalworking techniques. Chinese script became widespread.

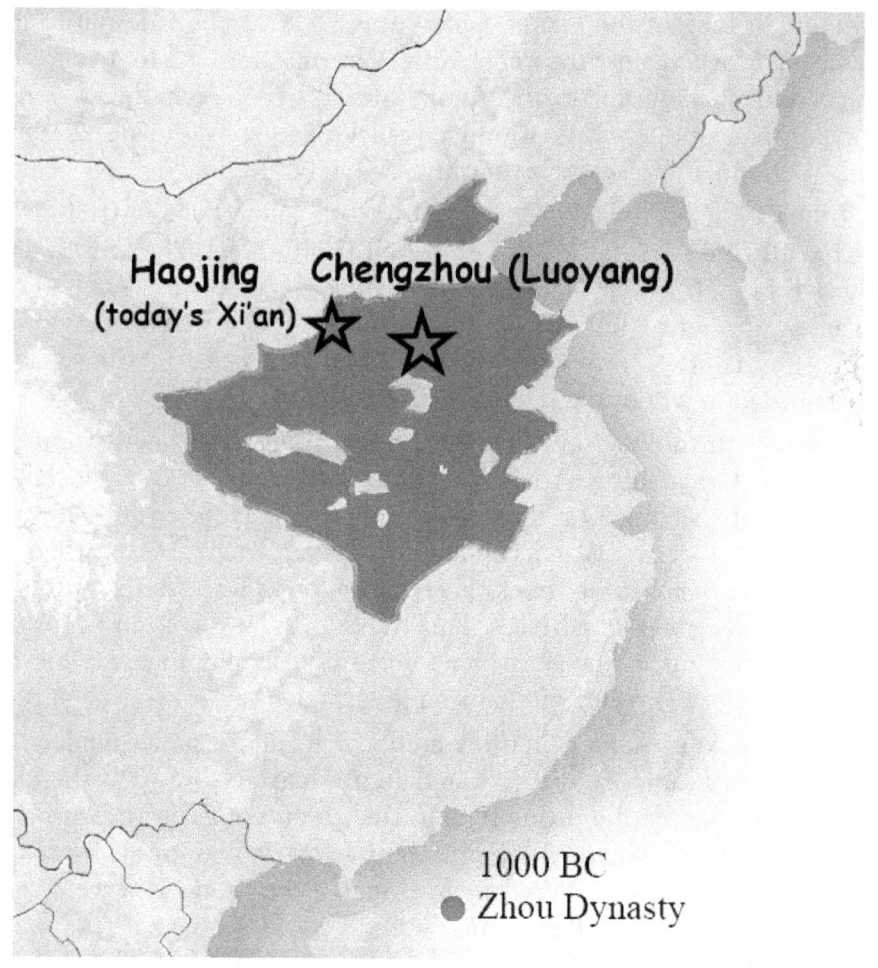

The Zhou dynasty with western and eastern capitals"

After three centuries, the vassal kings became increasingly powerful as the emperor's authority weakened. Politically, power shifted to the Eastern Zhou at the new capital of Chengzhou.

Despite the mayhem, the early Eastern Zhou era witnessed a cultural surge in poetry, music, and philosophy known as the Spring and Autumn period (772-476 BCE). This was when Master K'ung (Confucius) wrote (or edited) the *Spring and Autumn Annals* about the dukes of the regional state of Lu (his home province). It also tied to the history of other regions of the Zhou Empire. He used natural events, such as solar and lunar eclipses, to date his history.

Due to the philosophies Confucius and others such as Laozi (Lao Tzu) and Mozi developed during this period, it became known as the

"Hundred Schools of Thought." Confucius emphasized the importance of social harmony and taught that exceptional rulers fostered loyalty, respect, and morality. He believed everyone had a key role to play in society and should always strive to cultivate knowledge and righteous behavior. He promoted filial piety—respect, love, and obedience toward one's parents and ancestors. He had a "reverse" golden rule: "Whatever you do not wish to happen to you, do not do to others."

Laozi developed Daoism (Taoism). He believed that inaction and non-involvement in worldly things lead to oneness with Dao, the "way" that governs the universe. He thought one should live a simple life and let go of attachments. Only humble people can be wise. One should not try to force change but let events unfold naturally. One should also not resist change but embrace it, as change is inevitable.

Mozi lived in the Warring States period and taught the philosophy of Mohism. He believed a person should love everyone, regardless of whether they were family, friends, or total strangers. People should strive for what is best for everyone, not just themselves. He believed society should promote productivity by valuing labor and fostering efficiency. He hated warfare and felt that people should coexist peacefully, resolving conflicts through diplomacy.

Legalism also had roots in the Warring States era. It was almost the opposite of Confucianism, Daoism, and Mohism. Legalism taught that people are evil at their core. If left to their own devices, most people are corrupt and selfish. Thus, the government must strictly enforce laws for everyone, high and low, to keep them on the right path. People who do the right thing ought to be rewarded.

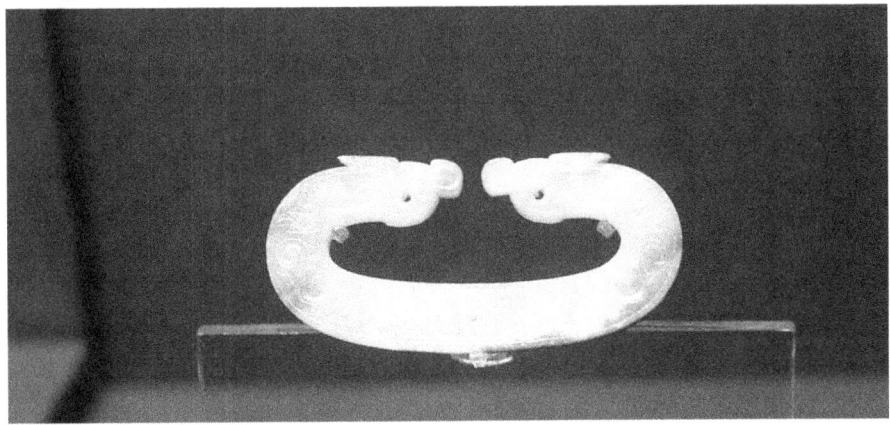

Eastern Zhou jade ornament [48]

After the Zhou dynasty relocated its capital to Luoyang, it continued a similar government model. However, the central government became weaker, while the vassal states grew stronger and more independent. As the imperial government broke down, people whispered that the Zhou dynasty had lost the Mandate of Heaven. The central government fragmented into feudal states. This led to the Warring States period (481–221 BCE), during which battles raged between the seven most powerful states, ultimately ending the Zhou dynasty. Despite turbulent times, intellectual growth and philosophical development continued unabated.

As the seven states fought each other, another threat came from the north and west. Horseback-riding nomadic tribes—including the Ordos, the Xianyun, and the Xiongnu—were crossing into China from the Russian and Mongolian steppes. The Chinese began building sections of packed earthen walls, about thirteen feet high, to keep them out. In the following Qin dynasty, Emperor Qin Shi Huang connected these sections into a unified wall.

The Xia, Shang, and Zhou dynasties left an enduring legacy in culture, government systems, philosophy, writing, technology, and many other areas. They set the stage for the unification of China under the Qin dynasty.

# Chapter 6: The Rise of the Hittites and the Assyrians

A sense of foreboding gripped the Babylonians. Two recent eclipses of the moon and the sun foretold their king would die, yet none of the usual enemies posed a threat. Then, they saw dust rising in the distance. Minutes later, a guard from the northern frontier charged in.

"It's the Hittites! Hordes of them! Get into the city! Shut the gates!"

"The Hittites? They're a thousand miles away!"

The Hittite Empire *was* a thousand miles away, yet their king, Mursili I, invaded Babylon in 1595 BCE. He had no interest in ruling Babylon. He wanted their wheat. The catastrophic volcanic eruption on the island of Thera had disrupted weather patterns, causing harvests to fail. Babylon was far enough away not to be affected much, and its irrigation farming ensured a consistent wheat surplus.

Before the Babylonians knew what was happening, the Hittites swooped in and enslaved most of the people. They stole the cult image of Babylon's chief god, Marduk, stripped the temples of their treasures, and emptied their storehouses of grain.

The formidable Hittites played a pivotal role in shaping the politics and culture of the Near East. They were among the first people, if not *the* first, to invent ironworking technology. Iron weapons gave them a significant edge. When they emerged in northern Mesopotamia by 1800 BCE, no one called them "Hittites." They called themselves the "people of Nesha," a place in central Anatolia (present-day Turkey) where they lived before migrating west.

The "Hittites" of ancient Turkey were not the Hittites in the Bible. The biblical Hittites lived in Canaan before, during, and after the Hittite Empire. So, how did the people in Anatolia get the name "Hittite?" Nineteenth-century archaeologists mistakenly identified the people of the Hatti Empire as the biblical Hittites. The incorrect name stuck.

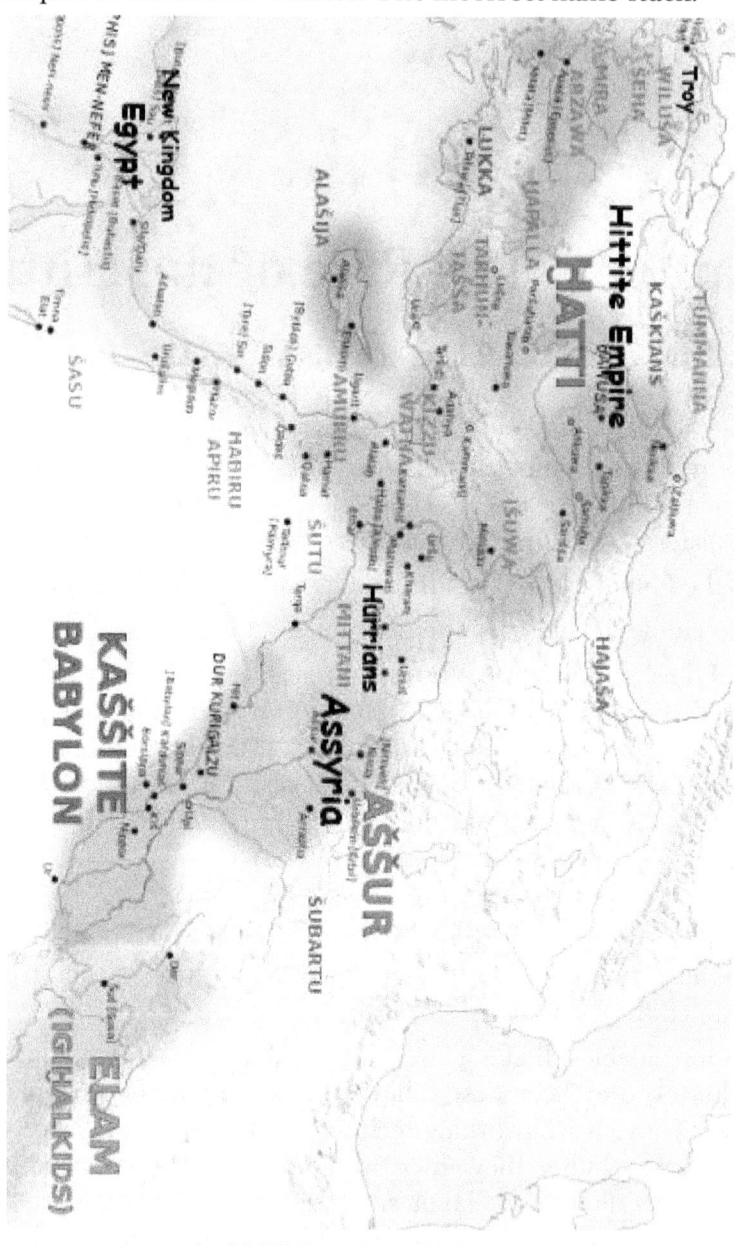

Middle East, circa 1300 BCE[a]

Where did the (non-biblical) Hittites come from? Their earliest written history places them in Kussara, in eastern Anatolia. The Hittite King Pithana conquered Kanesh (Nesha) in central Anatolia around 1780 BCE. It was a nighttime raid, and they did not kill anyone. His son, Anitta, recorded his father's exploits in the *Anitta Text*, the oldest known Hittite literature. The Hittites wrote in cuneiform, adopted from the Akkadians.

Around 1700 BCE, King Anitta invaded Hattusa in central Anatolia, the capital of the Hattian people. The Hittites burned the city, then left it abandoned. Fifty years later, Anitta's descendant, Hattusili I, rebuilt Hattusa and made it the new Hittite capital. It had colossal stone walls and a lion gate facing southwest—the one the Mycenaean Greeks copied. Two sphinxes guarded Hattusa's southern gate. Hattusa's archive held ten thousand tablets, shining a light on Hittite history.

Hattusa Sphinx Gate "

The Hurrians of the Mitanni kingdom were neighbors of the Hittites. They lived at the Hittites' southeastern border, west of the Assyrians. The Hittites translated and recorded Hurrian mythology, as well as other writings. One book the Hittites translated was a guide to training chariot horses. (The Hurrians perfected lightweight war chariots with spoked wheels.)

The Hittites had thousands of gods, but their chief deity was Tarhunt, the god of thunder, who ruled the heavens and the mountains. He was in perpetual conflict with Illuyanka, the serpent. Another important deity was Tarhunt's wife, Arinna (Wurušemu), the sun goddess.

Tarhum (Tarhunt), the Hittite god of thunder "

The Hittite king Šuppiluliuma I shattered the friendship with the Hurrians by launching a surprise attack. He conquered part of the Mitanni kingdom in 1344 BCE and made the Hurrian king a vassal under his rule.

At this time, Egypt controlled the Mediterranean coastline up to Syria. When Egypt's teenage pharaoh, Tutankhamun, unexpectedly died without an heir, his advisor, Ay, tried to usurp the throne. Part of his plan was coercing King Tut's widow, Ankhesenamun, to marry him. The widow snorted at the thought of marrying a non-royal. Instead, she reached out to Šuppiluliuma I, asking him to send one of his sons to marry her.

The Hittite king's jaw dropped when he read her letter. Whoever heard of a woman arranging her own marriage? Yet, he liked the idea of a son on Egypt's throne. He sent his son, Zannanza, to marry Ankhesenamun. Ay heard he was coming and killed the young Hittite prince. Enraged, Šuppiluliuma attacked Egyptian territory in Syria and Canaan—a fatal move. The Egyptian military was sick with either tularemia (rabbit fever) or the bubonic plague. The disease killed Šuppiluliuma I, his son Arnuwanda II, and much of the Hittite military.

In this era, the Hurrians, Hittites, Assyrians, Babylonians, and Egyptians were what modern scholars call the "Great Powers" of the Middle East. They occasionally fought each other, but they also arranged marriages between their royal families. They wrote letters back and forth, calling each other "brother."

Although fierce warriors, the Hittite kings were also skilled negotiators. The Hittites' Treaty of Kadesh with Egypt was one of the earliest peace treaties, showcasing the Hittites' sophisticated approach to law and diplomacy.

The famous Battle of Kadesh set the stage for this treaty. In 1274 BCE, Egypt's high-powered pharaoh, Ramesses II, charged north, determined to regain the territory lost to the Hittites. His target was Kadesh, a city in Syria that Egypt had ruled for 150 years. Now, the Hittites had it. As he neared Kadesh, Ramesses noticed two shepherds sitting in the shade.

"Do you know where the Hittites and their King Muwatalli are?"

"Far away!" the shepherds grinned. "Muwatalli was quivering in fear when he heard you were coming. He ran away to Aleppo."

Ramesses was so eager to capture Kadesh that he rushed off with only his advance unit of five thousand men and five hundred chariots, leaving the other three-quarters of his army far behind. Little did he know the shepherds were Muwatalli's misinformation agents. They tricked Ramesses into riding into a trap. The Hittite army was waiting for

Ramesses in Kadesh with 37,000 men and 3,000 chariots.

Most of the Hittites had iron spearheads and swords, far stronger than the bronze weapons the elite Egyptian warriors carried. Most Egyptian soldiers carried copper swords and spearheads, which were brittle and difficult to sharpen.

As Ramesses approached Kadesh, he paled when he saw the Hittites pouring out from behind a nearby mountain. He looked over his shoulder. Some of his men were wading across the Orontes River, while others were struggling up the hill toward the city. Vastly outnumbered, the Egyptian troops scattered as the Hittites charged. The Hittites encircled Ramesses with their chariots, cutting him off from his men.

However, the Egyptian chariots were easier to maneuver. Ramesses charged the Hittites, over and over, until he broke through their line. Sweat pouring from his brow, Ramesses grinned when he saw more of his men arriving. They pinned the Hittites between the other Egyptian units, then forced them into the river. Some escaped to safety on the other side, while others drowned.

Ramesses II's propaganda painting shows him pushing the Hittites into the Orontes River. "

Both sides declared victory. Ramesses II crowed, "We pushed the Hittites into the river!"

Hattusili III, Muwatalli's brother and the next Hittite king, called him out: "You failed to take Kadesh! Wasn't that the point?"

Hattusili and Ramesses mended fences and agreed to the "Eternal Peace Treaty," in which each promised not to attack or take the other's land.

Two years after the Battle of Kadesh, the Assyrian king Shalmaneser I launched an assault against the Hittites and Hurrians. He bragged about capturing tens of thousands and gouging out their eyes. The Hittites struggled through the next six decades and fell during the Bronze Age collapse. Drought led to food shortages. An earthquake storm rocked the region between 1225 and 1175 BCE. Internal strife, invasion by the Sea Peoples, and battles with Assyria led to the Hittites' downfall. However, their groundbreaking technology in iron manufacturing survived and changed the course of history.

The Assyrians of northern Mesopotamia built a spine-chilling reputation. Their advanced military technology and strategies, coupled with abject cruelty, struck terror among their foes.

But what were the origins of the Assyrians? How did they rise to power?

Semitic herders migrated into northern Iraq during the Sumerian era. Nineveh, built by the Hassuna civilization during the Neolithic Age, was already thriving on the eastern banks of the Tigris River. Most early Assyrians were nomadic herders, and their first seventeen chieftains lived in tents.

A man named Aššur (Ashur) built a city by the same name around 2600 BCE on the Tigris River's western banks. The chief Assyrian god also had the name Ashur. (They probably elevated their ancestor to god status.) Besides worshiping Ashur, the Assyrians erected temples to the goddess Ishtar and Adad, the Amorite rain god.

Ashur, the Assyrian founder and patron god [47]

Around 2025 BCE, Puzur-Ashur I launched the Old Assyrian Empire. Powerful kings expanded Assyrian territory into former Akkadian and Sumerian lands.

In 1808 BCE, King Šamši-Adad I of Terqa (in Syria) conquered Assyria. He claimed he had the right. "My ancestors were Assyrian chieftains!" Assyria became a true empire as it swept parts of Anatolia, Syria, Lebanon, and Canaan under its rule. Assyrian supremacy fell only six decades later. Mari (in Syria) and Eshnunna (in central Iraq) snatched all the lands Šamši-Adad I had annexed.

The Adaside dynasty began about 1700 BCE, launching Assyria into an era of strength and prosperity. In the 1400s BCE, Egypt's pharaoh Thutmose III conquered the coastline up to Syria. He then crossed the Euphrates and took the Mitanni kingdom. The Hurrians and Hittites fought together against the Egyptians. However, the Assyrians allied with Egypt, a deadly mistake. The furious Hurrian-Hittite forces launched a surprise attack on Assyria in 1430 BCE, wiping out the Old Assyrian Empire.

For thirty-eight years, the Assyrians paid tribute to the Hurrians while quietly rebuilding their strength. They smiled when the Hurrian-Hittite coalition frayed. Finally, in 1392 BCE, the Assyrian king Eriba-Adad I broke free from the Hurrians. The Middle Assyrian Empire launched, more dynamic than ever. Within decades, it snatched part of the Mitanni kingdom when a revolt rocked the Hurrians.

The Assyrian king Arik-den-ili (1317–1306 BCE) subdued the nomadic Aramean and Sutean tribes west of the Euphrates. He built the great ziggurat in Ashur. His son, Adad-nirari I, charged south, taking Babylonia's northern territory. He captured the Hurrian king, forcing him to swear loyalty. When the Hittite king Mursili I heard, he wrote an irate letter: "So, you have become a 'Great King,' have you? But why do you still talk about 'brotherhood?'"[5]

Shalmaneser I, who obliterated the Mitanni kingdom, began the Assyrian custom of population relocation. The Assyrians moved entire cities of rebellious conquered people to other provinces and resettled the cities with people from elsewhere. In the Neo-Assyrian period,

---

[5] Harry A. Hoffner, Jr., *Letters from the Hittite Kingdom: Writings from the Ancient World* (Atlanta: Society of Biblical Literature, 2009), 322–4.

Sargon II conquered northern Israel and deported over twenty-seven thousand Jews to Assyria. He resettled the Israeli towns with conquered people from Babylonia and Syria.

The Assyrian king Tukulti-Ninurta smashed the Hittites in 1245 BCE, enslaving twenty-eight thousand, bragging, "I filled the caves and ravines of the mountains with their corpses. I made heaps of their corpses like (grain) piles beside their gates. Their cities I destroyed, ravaged, and turned into ruin hills."[6]

A royal lion hunt in a relief in Nineveh [48]

Not only did Assyria survive the Bronze Age collapse, but King Tiglath-Pileser I (1114–1076 BCE) conquered the Phoenician cities of Tyre, Sidon, Berytus (Beirut), and Byblos. He rebuilt Assyria's temples and offered human sacrifices to the gods. Tiglath-Pileser bragged of killing fourteen elephants and nearly a thousand lions, both of which lived in the Middle East in those days.

The rulers after Tiglath-Pileser lost the lands he had conquered. Assyria shrank to its original homeland, and the Middle Assyrian Empire ended in 1055 BCE.

---

[6] *The Great Inscription of Tukulti-Ninurta I*, trans. Yigal Bloch (Omnika). https://omnika.org/texts/626

The Neo-Assyrian Empire leaped into action in 911 BCE with Adad-nirari II. It expanded into the largest empire the world had yet seen. The Assyrians' virtually unbeatable military machine, renowned for its brutality, struck fear across the Middle East.

The Neo-Hittite King Suppiluliuma [49]

Adad-nirari marched into Anatolia, petrifying the Neo-Hittites, who were disrupting Assyrian trade routes. Who were the Neo-Hittites? Some were the Luwian people who had lived in the Hittite Empire before it fell. Scholars believe they shared the same mother tongue as the Hittites.

Next, Adad-nirari swept into Babylonia, plundering the city's incredible wealth and using it to rebuild Assyria's military with the latest iron weapons and siege technology. Their deadly siege engines enabled them to get through or over the thick walls of the cities they attacked. Some siege engines had iron battering rams. Others were tall towers on wheels that the Assyrians used to launch arrows into the city. They could also throw up portable ladders from their wheeled towers and climb into the city.

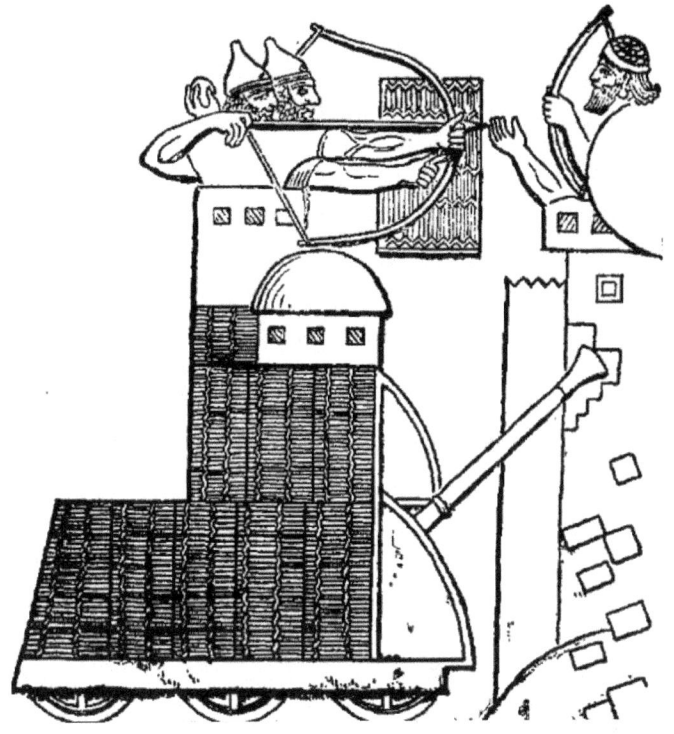

This wheeled siege engine in a drawing of an Assyrian relief has both a battering ram and a tower from which to shoot arrows into the city.[50]

Assyrian engineers also dug underneath the city walls, causing them to fall down. Another tactic was diverting irrigation canals to flood the city.

The Assyrians peeled the skin off of captured soldiers or impaled them on stakes in view of horrified onlookers from the walls. These shock and terror tactics often impelled cities to surrender immediately when the Assyrians attacked, rather than suffer such atrocities.

Tukulti-Ninurta II (890-884 BCE) subdued the Medes and Persians of ancient Iran. They had to pay tribute of horses, camels, copper, gold, and iron to Assyria. Controlling the Medes and Persians also meant access to the Great Khorasan Road, which ran from Babylon into Central Asia. It was part of the Silk Road to China, bringing unimaginable riches in trade.

Ashurnasirpal II (883-859 BCE), the son of Tukulti-Ninurta, savagely conquered parts of Anatolia and Syria. He bragged about cutting the heads off eight hundred soldiers and burning the teen boys. He impaled five hundred soldiers and built a pile of heads at the city gate. His son, Shalmaneser III (859-824 BCE), defeated Babylon, an epic win that gave the Assyrians control of all Mesopotamia. Yet, a coalition of nations gathered to fight him.

On the Kurkh Monoliths, Shalmaneser III described the 853 BCE Battle of Qarqar. It was the largest battle in Middle Eastern history to that point. In the inscription, Shalmaneser said he was making his annual tour of his conquered lands. When he reached Hamath in west-central Syria, pandemonium broke out. The Luwian people resisted, so he trashed their palaces and city.

As he left Hamath, a massive coalition confronted him. King Ahab of Israel, King Hadadezer of Damascus, and King Irhuleni of Hamath were waiting for him. With them were the Arabians, Jordanians, Lebanese, and Neo-Hittites. He said that 52,000 infantry, 3,900 chariots, 1,900 cavalry, and 1,000 men on camels covered the plain.

Of course, Shalmaneser claimed victory on his monument, saying he killed 14,000 men, while none of the other kings lost their lives or thrones. No doubt, he consolidated his control over Syria and Israel. Several years later, the Assyrian Black Obelisk pillar pictured King Jehu of Israel presenting tribute to Shalmaneser.

King Jehu of Israel bows before Shalmaneser III on the Black Obelisk carving [31]

Through its sophisticated administration, advanced siege technology, and nearly invincible military, the Neo-Assyrian Empire reached its greatest extent around 670 BCE, following King Esarhaddon's conquest of Egypt. It stretched from the Zagros Mountains in the east to Egypt in the southwest and Anatolia in the north.

The Neo-Assyrian king Ashurbanipal (668–627 BCE) built the sensational Library of Ashurbanipal in Nineveh. It was not the world's first library, but it was the first to systematically organize a mind-boggling collection of tablets from around the known world. The library preserved not only Assyrian works but also the history and literature of the Sumerians, Akkadians, Babylonians, and other ancient civilizations. It was a repository of Mesopotamian literature, science, and history.

Sadly, the majestic library, which housed approximately thirty thousand tablets, stood for only about three decades before the Medes and Babylonians sacked and burned Nineveh. However, thousands of the clay tablets survived, buried under the rubble, and were uncovered by archaeologists Sir Austen Henry Layard and Hormuzd Rassam in the 1850s CE.

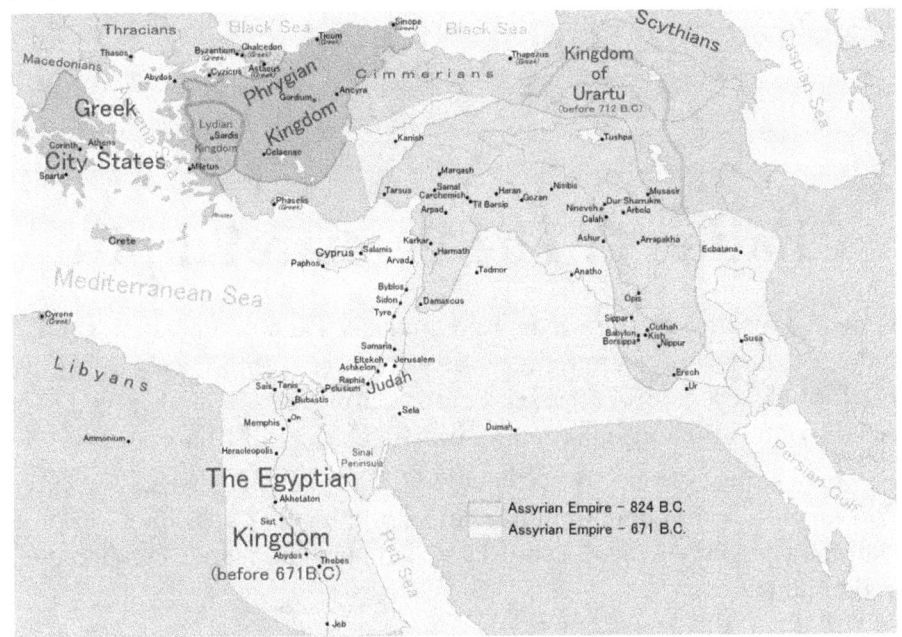

The Neo-Assyrian Empire at its height in 671 BCE.⁵³

Conquering and creating the world's largest empire was one thing. Maintaining it proved impossible, especially after a catastrophic drought and a military revolt exacerbated the situation. In 612 BCE, the Babylonians, Medes, Persians, Chaldeans, Scythians, and Cimmerians plotted their revenge against the Assyrians' vicious inhumanity. Their sheer numbers were staggering.

After the capital of Nineveh fell, the Medes killed King Sinsharishkun. The royal family fled to Harran in Anatolia and desperately messaged the Egyptian pharaoh Necho for help. He marched north, but King Josiah of Judah stood in his way. Necho killed Josiah, but the delay allowed the Babylonians and Medes to break into Harran. Necho arrived too late to save the Assyrians. Then, to his horror, the Babylonian crown prince Nebuchadnezzar II wiped out the Egyptian army.

# Chapter 7: The Persian Empire

When Cyrus the Great took the reins, ancient Persia's unassuming realm suddenly mushroomed into the globe's first mega-empire, covering a vast swath of Central and West Asia. Under Darius the Great, it spread over an area of two million square miles in Asia, Africa, and Europe.

This chapter covers the Achaemenid Empire, the first of the three Persian empires. Where did this name come from? Cyrus the Great and Darius I claimed an eighth-century Persian chieftain named Achaemenes as their ancestor.

Where did it all begin? Persia emerged as a small kingdom where today's Fars province lies in southwestern Iran. "Soft lands breed soft people," Cyrus the Great once said. His homeland was certainly not soft. It lay on the rugged Iranian Plateau, bordered by the jagged Zagros Mountains and the desolate Lut and Kavir salt deserts. The name "Iran" originates from "Aryan," which means "free and noble" in the Indo-Iranian language of Cyrus's ancestors, who once inhabited the regions of today's Afghanistan, Turkmenistan, and Uzbekistan. Around 1500 BCE, the Aryan migration spread these Indo-Iranian tribes south and west. One group arrived in northern Iran about 1100 BCE and established the Median Kingdom. Another group speaking "Old Persian" arrived in southwestern Iran, where the ancient Elamites lived.

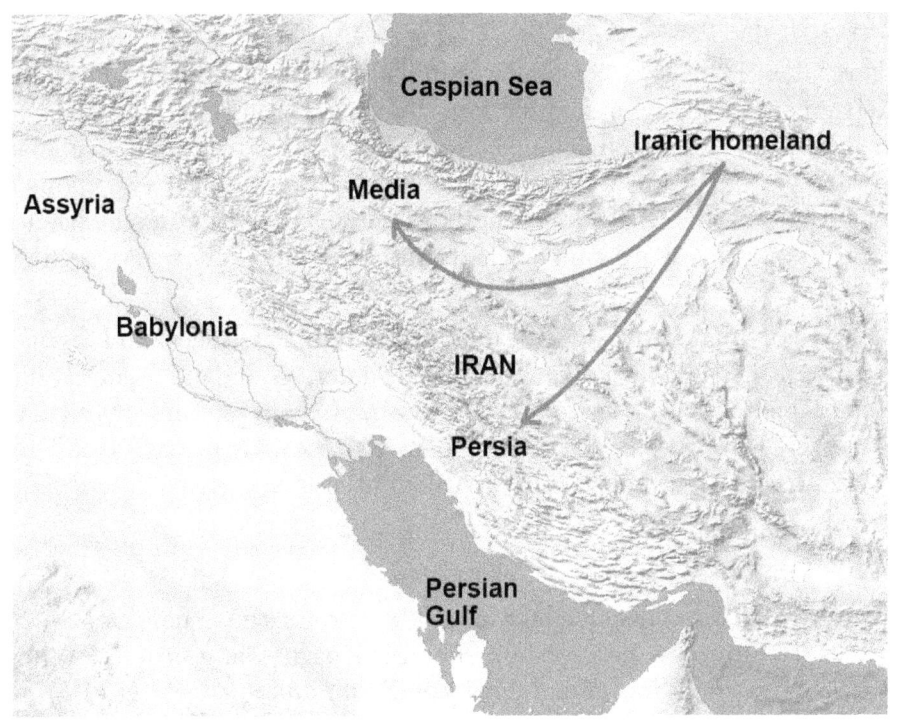

Indo-Iranic Migration of Medes and Persians [58]

The Persians lived alongside the Elamites, adopting their cuneiform script. Iran was a part of the Neo-Assyrian Empire at that time. The Assyrian King Shalmaneser III wrote on the "Black Obelisk" in 836 BCE that he received tribute from twenty-seven Persian kings (probably tribal chieftains). The Persians were renowned for the horses they bred, so Assyrian kings demanded horses as tribute payments.

When the Medes and Persians resisted the Assyrians, the Assyrian king Tiglath-Pileser III (745-727 BCE) deported 65,000 Medes to Syria and imported Phoenicians and Syrians to northern Iran. He did not relocate the Persians, but he cut off the thumbs of the men's right hands so they could not wield weapons.

Like most Indo-Iranian tribes, the early Persians rarely created cult images. They offered sacrifices to their ancestors and worshiped outdoors in their nomadic days. Later, they built simple temples with perpetual fires burning. They sacrificed horses and worshipped the gods of the Vedic religion, prevalent among the Indo-Iranian people. Early Persian religious rituals included drinking haoma, derived from the soma plant, to receive enlightenment and draw closer to the divine. They also poured out haoma as an offering to the gods.

When the Persians first migrated into Iran, they were independent clans. Teispes (Cyrus's great-grandfather), the founder of the Achaemenid dynasty, united the Persian clans. Darius the Great claimed that he also descended from Teispes, but from a different line than Cyrus. Teispes's son, Cyrus I (grandfather of Cyrus the Great), joined the coalition forces that wiped out the Assyrians. At that time, the Medes were the strongest tribe in ancient Iran, and the Persians were their vassals.

Cyrus I made a treaty with the Median King Astyages, and Cyrus's son, Cambyses, married Astyages's daughter, Mandane. The young couple had a baby, Cyrus II (Cyrus the Great), around 600 BCE. However, King Astyages had a nightmare that Cyrus would capsize his kingdom. Highly agitated, Astyages called his astrologers.

"What should I do?" he asked.

"You must kill the baby!" they insisted.

Astyages invited his daughter to visit him so that he could see his new grandson. However, he gave his general Harpagus these orders: "When Mandane isn't looking, grab the baby and kill him!"

Harpagus snatched the infant, but instead of killing him, he gave him to Mithradates, the cowherd, whose newborn son had just died. King Astyages found out that his grandson was still alive when Cyrus was ten years old.

"The omen has passed! The boy is no longer a danger to you," his astrologers assured him.

Astyages sent Cyrus back to Persia to live with his birth parents. Yet, he often invited his grandson to visit him. When Cyrus became a teenager, Astyages taught him the art of war and made him one of his generals. Around 559 BCE, Cyrus's father died, and he became king of Persia. As a vassal king under his grandfather, Cyrus paid tribute and provided soldiers for the Median army. However, the warm relationship between Cyrus and his Median grandfather soured. His grandfather was forcing the Persian farmers into slave labor.

The Median general Harpagus, who had saved Cyrus as a baby, messaged him. "March out with your men against your grandfather. My troops will abandon him and join you," he told Cyrus.

Harpagus hated Astyages because the king had killed Harpagus's son when he discovered Harpagus had spared the infant Cyrus.

The Median soldiers handed King Astyages over to Cyrus, who spared his life. Cyrus became the ruler of the massive Median Empire, stretching from the Arabian Sea to the Black Sea. But Cyrus was only getting started. Cyrus's next target was Sardis, the capital of Lydia in western Anatolia. Its king, the wealthy Croesus, had captured a Median city in Cappadocia and enslaved its people. Croesus turned pale as 196,000 Medes and Persians approached, the ground shaking under their horses' hooves.

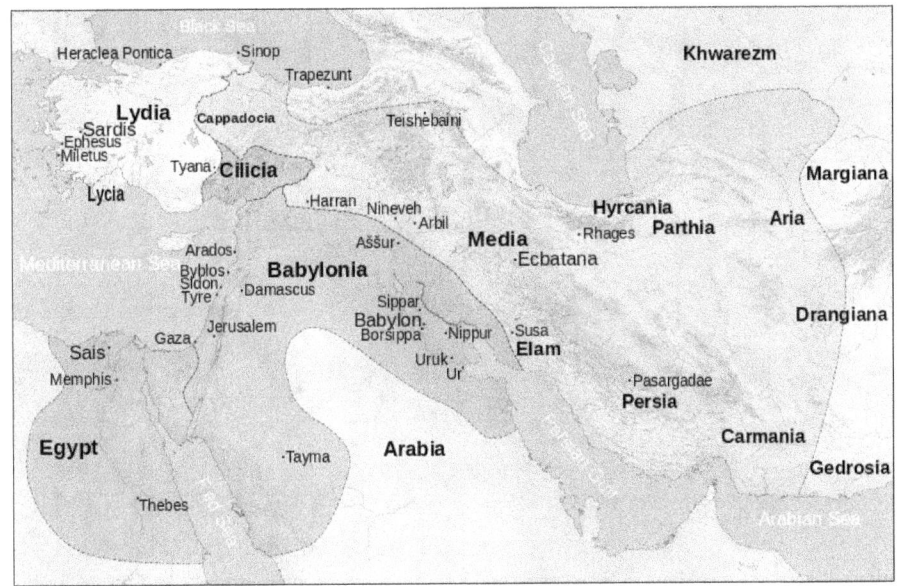

The Median Empire at its height⁴

"I still have twice as many men!" Croesus muttered to himself.

General Harpagus came to Cyrus's aid once again, telling him, "Put your three hundred camels on your front line!"

They were pack animals, not war camels. Yet, Croesus's warhorses had never encountered camels—or smelled their musky odor. They reared up and raced off. The Lydians dashed inside the city walls, yet Cyrus deployed his siege towers, from which his archers released fiery arrows into the city. Sardis fell in two weeks.

Cyrus attempted to execute Croesus by burning; however, a timely rainstorm extinguished the fire. Croesus dusted himself off and dryly remarked, "Tell your men to stop ransacking the city."

"Why?"

"It's your city now! Why let them ruin it?"

Cyrus laughed and appointed Croesus as his advisor. General Harpagus and the Median army then conquered Ionia, a region of ancient Greek colonies on Anatolia's west coast. The mainland Greeks gasped when they heard how swiftly Ionia fell. Harpagus let the Ionians continue to self-rule, except they had to provide military men for Cyrus's war machine and pay tribute.

Alternating Persian soldiers in long gowns and Median warriors in short tunics and boots, from a bas relief at the Persepolis Apadana [55]

Meanwhile, Cyrus charged east to present-day Uzbekistan to conquer the Sogdians. With that accomplished, he headed to the Phoenician cities on Lebanon's coast. Tyre, Sidon, Byblos, and Tripoli pragmatically surrendered immediately. Cyrus only required them to pay a portion of 350 talents of silver annually (Syria, Judah, and Cyprus paid the rest.) Cyrus needed a navy for his long-term goals, and the Phoenicians were exceptional shipbuilders and sailors.

When Cyrus became king of the Medes and Persians, King Nabonidus of Babylon had been sulking in the desert for a decade. He was not meant to rule. Nabonidus was a descendant of the Assyrian king Ashurbanipal. After Harran fell, Nebuchadnezzar II brought the child Nabonidus and his mother back with him to Babylon, where Nabonidus served as a courtier. His son, Belshazzar, had staged a palace coup and put him on the throne.

Nabonidus was more interested in religion than running an empire. When the Babylonians resisted his religious reforms, Nabonidus left Belshazzar as his regent and abandoned Babylon. However, news of Tyre surrendering to Cyrus stirred Nabonidus. It had taken Nebuchadnezzar II thirteen years to conquer Tyre. Nabonidus could not let the Persians have it! He hurried back to Babylon.

When Nabonidus heard Cyrus was marching toward Babylon's northern border, he marched to meet him, leaving Belshazzar in charge of Babylon. Nebuchadnezzar had built a wall stretching from the Tigris to the Euphrates River to keep the Medes out of Babylon. The cities of Opis (on the Tigris) and Sippar (on the Euphrates) were at each end of the wall. Nabonidus stationed himself at Sippar.

Cyrus and his general, Gubaru the Mede, approached Opis in late September 539 BCE when the rivers were at their lowest. The Medes and Persians overcame the Babylonian forces stationed at Opis. Then, the Persian engineers diverted the Tigris into irrigation canals, lowering the river level until it was knee deep. Once his army crossed the river, Cyrus sent Gubaru and half his men south to Babylon.

Cyrus led the rest of his army to Sippar, which surrendered without a fight. Shocked, King Nabonidus slipped out of Sippar and raced toward Babylon, which was celebrating a festival honoring Sin, the moon god. The Babylonians had no idea Cyrus had bypassed the barrier wall by wading across the river. General Gubaru reached Babylon in the dead of night. The Babylonians were drunkenly dancing in the streets, unaware of the danger that loomed. Belshazzar, the regent, was hosting a dinner for a thousand nobles, drinking from the silver and gold goblets that Nebuchadnezzar II had pilfered from Jerusalem's temple.

The biblical book of Daniel says that Belshazzar suddenly looked up in horror to see disembodied fingers writing on the wall. He called for his astrologers, but no one could read the writing. Then, the queen (Nabonidus's wife) strode into the banquet hall. "Call for Daniel," she said. "He will give you the interpretation. He has insight, intelligence, and wisdom like that of the gods."

Nebuchadnezzar II had brought some royal boys from Jerusalem, including Daniel, when he conquered the city. Now an old man, Daniel, entered the banquet hall and said, "The writing on the wall says, 'MENE, MENE, TEKEL, PARSIN.' It means you have been weighed on the scales and found lacking. Your kingdom is given over to the Medes and Persians" (Daniel 5).

As Daniel spoke, General Gubaru's army arrived on the other side of the Euphrates River from Babylon. Once again, his engineers diverted the river into the irrigation canals, and the military waded across. Xenophon, a fourth-century Greek historian, wrote that the Medes swept through the city to the king's palace, where Belshazzar stood in the banquet hall, his scimitar in his hand. They killed Belshazzar and all the nobles. Nabonidus was captured when he arrived two days later. However, Cyrus spared his life and sent him to govern the province of Carmania in Persia.

One of Cyrus's first acts was to undo the population-relocation policy of the Assyrians and Babylonians. All the Syrians, Medes, Jews, and other deported people could return to their homelands. Cyrus continued conquering until his mega-empire stretched from Afghanistan to the Mediterranean Sea. The Royal Road spanned fifteen hundred miles from Susa in Persia to Sardis, enabling the empire's efficient postal system to deliver a message from one end of the empire to the other in one week.

The Cyrus Cylinder, a summary of his reign[66]

Cyrus ruled with tolerance and respect for the religions of conquered peoples. He honored the Babylonian chief god Marduk and rebuilt the Jewish temple in Jerusalem. He also allowed local governments a high level of autonomy. His policies led to a thriving economy, loyalty, and stability. On the "Cyrus Cylinder," he inscribed his genealogy and how he captured Babylon, restored temples, corrected injustices, and released deported people to return home.

Cyrus permitted most conquered kings and governors to retain their positions as long as they remained loyal. He preserved the social order and customs of conquered lands. Cyrus appointed twenty-six satraps (governors) to rule the "satrapies" (provinces) of the empire. The satraps collected taxes, judged court cases, and maintained the road system. The empire introduced a uniform monetary system and standardized weights and measures. Cyrus's royal inspector, called the "King's Eye," helped him spy out corruption or brewing rebellions. His legal system had standardized laws and required evidence to convict a person. Even a woman could be a witness in court, something unheard of in ancient times.

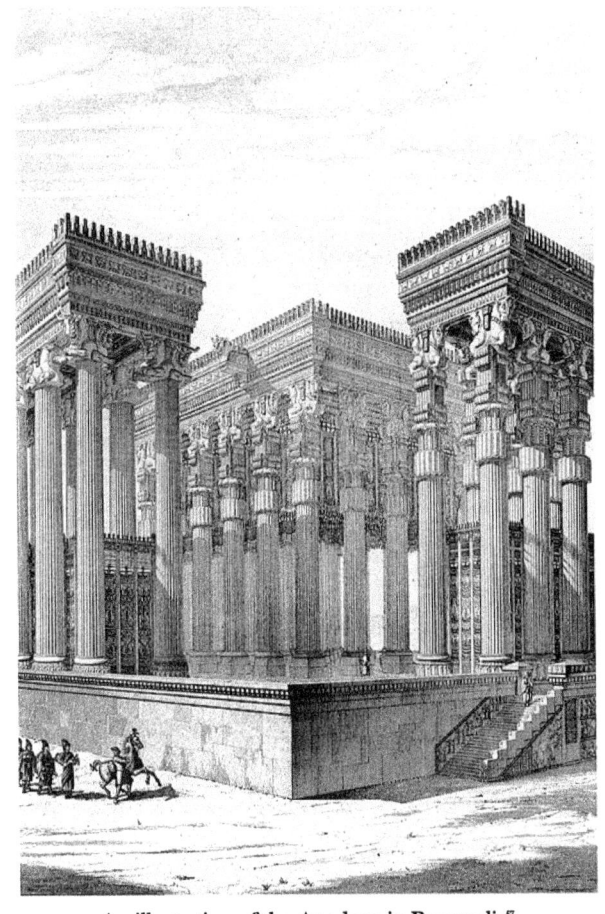

An illustration of the Apadana in Persepolis[87]

Cyrus the Great chose Persepolis, surrounded by the Zagros Mountains of Persia, as his ceremonial capital. He planned the city, but Darius the Great initiated the building project. Other kings continued building. Magnificent sixty-five-foot columns supported the roof of the luxurious king's hall, called the Apadana. At the eastern and northern ends, staircases featured bas-reliefs of various ethnicities from the empire bringing tribute, including a hippopotamus from Egypt.

After all his glorious triumphs, a woman named Tomyris killed Cyrus. She ruled over the Massagetae, a branch of the Scythes, another Indo-Iranian group. They were launching raids on Persia's northern borders. Cyrus thought he could tame the troublemakers by marrying their queen, but Tomyris rejected his overtures. In the ensuing bloodbath, she killed the seventy-year-old king in 530 BCE.

Cyrus's son, Cambyses, assumed the throne and conquered North Africa and Cyprus. While he was organizing Egypt's administration, word came of an uprising in Persia. While rushing home, he accidentally stabbed himself in the thigh. The wound developed gangrene, and he died of septic shock in 522 BCE. At least, that was the story Darius, his lance bearer, told everyone. Since Cambyses had no children, the next in line to the throne was his brother, Bardiya. However, Bardiya died mysteriously at about the same time. No descendants of Cyrus were left.

Bas relief of Darius I [58]

At that point, Darius, the lance bearer, claimed royal blood, announcing that he was also a descendant of Achaemenes, Cyrus's ancestor. Many were skeptical, but Darius furiously eliminated anyone who questioned his right to be "king of kings." Although likely a pretender to the throne, he took the Persian Empire to glorious new heights, the largest empire yet seen.

Darius the Great expanded into northern India's Punjab region, then subdued the Scythes who had killed Cyrus. He built a pontoon bridge over the Bosphorus Strait, which separates Asia from Europe, and crossed over to subdue Thrace (present-day Bulgaria) and Macedonia. Thrace was to be his staging area for conquering Greece.

A brilliant relief of a unicorn in the Apadana that Darius the Great built in Susa.[59]

In 499 BCE, the tyrant Histiaeus of Miletus spurred the Greeks of Ionia to rise in rebellion, allied with Athens and Eretria in southern Greece. However, their infighting and Darius's larger navy, commanded by General Mardonius, proved the Ionian Greeks' undoing. In 492, the Persians headed to Greece to punish Athens and Eretria. They were supposed to march through Thrace and into Greece, but their plans went awry. First, the Byrgi tribe attacked the land army. Although the Persians won, they were too weakened to battle the Greeks, leading to their retreat to Persia. Meanwhile, a diabolical storm sank three hundred vessels and killed twenty thousand men in the Persian navy headed to Greece.

Two years later, Darius organized a new army and navy to take on Greece. He had already sent ambassadors to Greece, ordering them to surrender to Persia or face his wrath. All the Greek city-states accepted Darius's demands, except Athens and its neighbor, Eretria.

"It's always the Athenians!" Darius fumed. "They and the Eritreans sent ships to aid the Ionian revolt. They will pay the price!"

Darius launched six hundred triremes (battleships) toward Greece. When the people of Eretria saw the Persian ships approaching on the horizon, most of them fled to Mount Olympus. However, two defectors opened the city gates. The Persians grabbed all the treasures they could carry, burned the city's temples, and enslaved anyone still in the city. Then, they sailed to Athens.

DATIS.          KALLIMACHOS.

General Datis of Persia fights the Greek Kallimachos in a drawing of the 460 BCE Painted Portico in Athens. [60]

Instead of waiting for the Persians to lay siege to their city, the Athenians marched across the peninsula to fight the Persians at Marathon. What the Persians did not know was that Marathon had mud pits that could swallow a person alive. It was also swampy, with mountain ridges reaching the sea. The Persians could not use their cavalry on the terrain.

The Greeks lined up on the side of a mountain. As the Persians approached, they ran full speed down the incline and crashed into the Persian forces before the Persian archers could shoot many arrows. The Persian soldiers broke through the Greek middle line, but the Greeks on the flanks encircled them. Panicked, the Persians turned and made a mad dash for the beach, some falling into the mud pits, never to be seen again. The Persians lost 6,400 men, but the Greeks only lost 203.

Darius seethed at the ignominious loss, vowing he would get revenge. Yet, his unexpected death meant that his son, Xerxes, inherited the throne and the quest for vengeance against Greece: "I will not rest until I have burned Athens to the ground!"

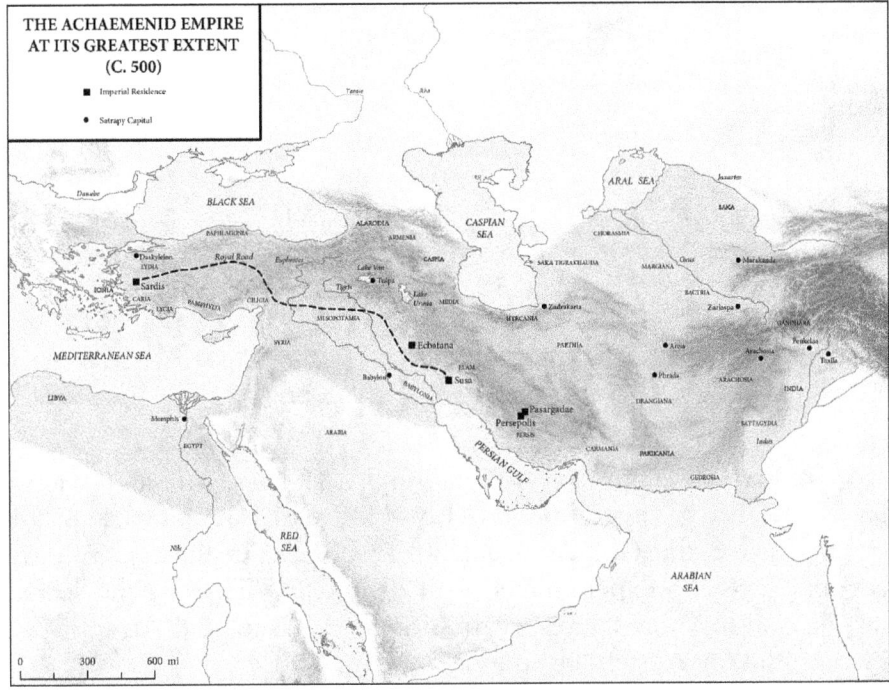

Achaemenid Empire under Darius I. The Royal Road stretched from Susa to Sardis.[61]

# Chapter 8: The Golden Age of Classical Greece

Extraordinary developments in philosophy, politics, art, and science marked Greece's Classical period (499-323 BCE). The pinnacle of this vibrant era was the Golden Age (480-423 BCE). In these glory days, dynamic city-states experimented with democracy. Thriving intellectual pursuits and towering figures, such as Socrates, Plato, and Aristotle, left their imprint on Western civilization.

Greece's Golden Age launched when the Greeks scored a major victory against Persia in 480 BCE. The Persian king of kings, Xerxes I, marched out with his million-man army, planning to cross the Dardanelles Strait into Europe using a pontoon bridge. Xerxes's engineers lashed 674 shallow boats together over the one-mile span, then built planking over them. However, a violent squall blew the bridge to pieces. Xerxes erupted in fury. He beheaded his engineers and even punished the water—three hundred lashes!

Finally, a new team of engineers reassembled the bridge, and the million-man army crossed over into Europe while the Persian navy sailed along the coast. Did Xerxes's army really have a million men? The Greek historian Herodotus, who lived in the Persian Empire at the time, insisted there were 2.5 million. Ctesias, a physician to Persian royalty about eight decades later, stated that Persia had 800,000 soldiers, along with support personnel. Still, the logistical challenges of managing and feeding a million men moving through enemy territory strain credibility.

As Xerxes marched into Greece, the northern and central Greek city-states offered no resistance. The Athenians in southern Greece knew they were Xerxes's target and were relieved when Sparta allied with them. Usually, the two cities were rivals.

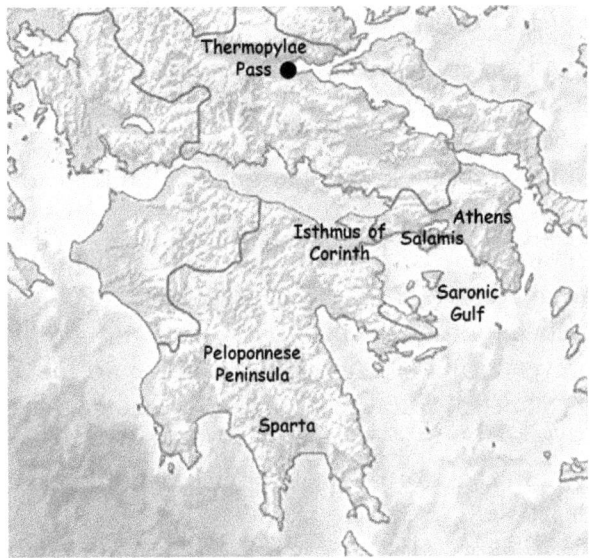

Southern Greece [62]

To reach southern Greece, the Persians had to march through the narrow Thermopylae pass between the Malian Gulf and Mount Kallidromo. A crumbling ancient wall ran from the gulf to the mountain. That is where seven thousand men from Sparta and Thebes awaited them, led by Sparta's King Leonidas. They had been repairing the defensive wall. Could they hold off Xerxes's massive army?

The Greeks stood shoulder to shoulder in the classic Greek phalanx formation. Their shields overlapped slightly, forming a defensive wall. The men behind the front line held their shields over their heads, creating a protective ceiling from arrows. Each man on the front line held an eight-foot spear, pointing toward the enemy.

Xerxes unleashed his ten thousand "Immortals," Persia's deadliest forces, against the Greeks. Yet the Spartans, renowned for their rigid discipline, stood firm for two days. If a soldier fell, the one behind him stepped into his place. The Persian archers shot volleys of arrows that darkened the sky, but they bounced off the Greeks' shield "ceiling."

On the third day, a Greek shepherd, hoping for a reward from Xerxes, showed the Persians a narrow path over the mountain.

A contingent of Immortals climbed the path and went down the other side, to the rear of the Greeks. King Leonidas ordered a unit to attack the Persians approaching their rear. He instructed most of the soldiers to withdraw to southern Greece to protect the Peloponnesian Peninsula.

King Leonidas and 1,400 men held off the Persians while the rest of the men escaped. Eventually, more Immortals crossed the shepherds' pass and attacked the Greeks from behind. Hundreds of thousands of Persians pressed in from the front, killing every Greek left in the pass, including Leonidas. Their sacrifice permitted a future victory for Greece.

Meanwhile, the Persian navy, with 1,200 ships, sailed down the Aegean Sea toward Athens. A fierce storm sank one-third of the fleet off northern Greece's coast of Magnesia. The Athenian and Corinthian navies were waiting for them at the Straits of Artemisium. For three days, the Greeks prevented the Persians from sailing into the Euboean Gulf and down the Straits of Euboea. Some Persian ships headed south on the open sea, where another storm sank two hundred ships. The Greeks cheered at the news that storms had sunk half of the Persian fleet.

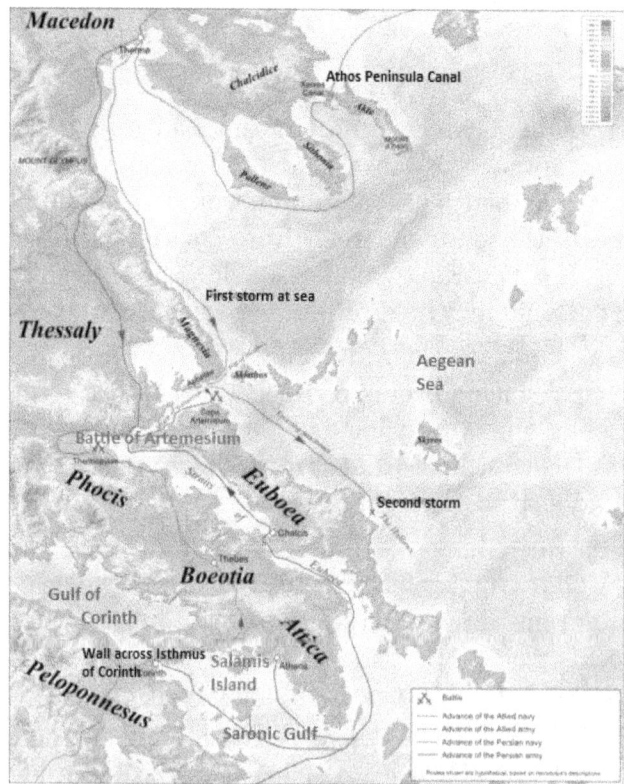

Progress of Xerxes' navy [68]

Athens' navy raced to the Saronic Gulf, desperate to get there before the Persian ships. They evacuated Athens' population to the island of Salamis in the Saronic Gulf. Fleets from Sparta, Corinth, and Macedonia gathered at Salamis. Meanwhile, Xerxes's army approached the Peloponnese Peninsula. The delay at Thermopylae enabled the Spartans, Corinthians, and other Greeks on the Peloponnese Peninsula to finish rebuilding a four-mile ancient wall on the Isthmus of Corinth, blocking entry to the peninsula.

Xerxes marched to Athens first, eager to settle old scores. He entered the ancient city unhindered and killed the few people left. The Persians ransacked Athens and reduced its elegant temples on the Acropolis to ashes. Xerxes then led his men toward the Peloponnese Peninsula to get revenge on Sparta. However, the rebuilt, heavily guarded wall blocked the Isthmus of Corinth. Xerxes muttered curses as he laid siege to the wall.

Meanwhile, the leaders of Athens, Corinth, and Sparta held a war council at Salamis. They worried about Xerxes getting through the wall. He would devastate Sparta, Corinth, and the other cities on the peninsula.

"Let's distract Xerxes! Bring him here—to Salamis!" said Athens's naval commander, Themistocles, leaning forward eagerly. "He only has about six hundred ships left. Our Athenian navy just proved ourselves against his navy at Artemisium—and they had almost twice the ships! He doesn't know your navies are here. Together, we can beat him!"

The others frowned. "If we lure him here, we're endangering our women and children. We brought them to Salamis for safety."

"They will be safe," Themistocles insisted. "The Persians are better fighters on the open sea, but we've proved our superiority in tight places. We'll ambush him in the straits between Salamis and the mainland!"

The plan was daring and terrifying. Yet, the Greeks agreed to it. First, they needed to lure Xerxes's navy to Salamis. Themistocles messaged Xerxes, telling him he was clandestinely on the Persian side: "The rest of the Greeks are panicking. They're arguing among themselves, almost coming to blows. The Spartans are sailing home to protect their city. Send your fleet here to Salamis. We'll join our navies and conquer Greece together!"

Xerxes eagerly sent his navy to the Saronic Gulf. He ordered his men to carry his portable throne to the top of a mountain overlooking the gulf, where he could watch the battle. All the Greek ships, except fifty Corinthian vessels, hid behind Georgios Island. When the Persian navy arrived, they only saw the Corinthian ships, which turned and fled into the strait between Salamis and the mainland. The Persians chased them right into the trap.

The Persians heard an eerie sound wafting over the water. It was men singing a hymn to Apollo! Then they saw them. Hundreds of Greek battleships sailed around the bend of the island, blocking the Persian fleet in the strait. The Greeks struck the trapped Persian vessels over and over with their battering rams. Dead bodies and ship wreckage covered the water. Watching the carnage from the mountain above, Xerxes turned white. The war on Greece was over, for now. The Greeks had sunk his navy, and he was running out of food and supplies for his army.

Sea Battle of Salamis[64]

The battles against the Persian Empire united the southern Greek city-states against a common foe, fostering a sense of shared Hellenic identity. Collectively, they were on the offensive against Persia. Collaboration had been the key to winning the war. If they wanted to end the Persian threat permanently, they needed to continue working as a team.

The victory at Salamis encouraged several Greek city-states in Ionia to rebel, assisted by the Spartans and Athenians. In a spectacular victory, the Greeks seized control of the Aegean Sea. However, the Spartans predicted the Persians would try to retake Ionia. "The Ionian Greeks should move to mainland Greece!" they suggested.

The Ionians responded angrily, "We've lived here for centuries! We're not leaving!"

The Athenians agreed. "Our ancestors established these colonies. We can't let the Persians have them! We will form a league to protect the Aegean Sea."

Thus, 330 Greek cities surrounding the Aegean Sea formed the Delian League in 478 BCE, with Cimon, a hero of the Battle of Salamis, as its naval commander. The cities in the league donated ships, crews, or funding to keep the Persians out of the Aegean. When the Persians rebuilt their navy and attacked Pamphylia, Cimon sank two hundred Persian warships. The Persians dared not enter the Aegean for the next fifteen years. The Delian League also ejected the pirates from the Aegean.

In 460 BCE, Egypt rebelled against Persia. Pericles, a rising star in Athens, led 250 ships of the Delian League to help the Egyptians gain independence. It was a disaster for the Greeks, who lost twenty thousand men and most of their ships.

Initially, the Delian League's treasury was at the sacred island of Delos in the Aegean. Pericles expressed concern that the Persians might raid the small island and take it. He moved the treasury to Athens, ostensibly for safekeeping. So, when the Greeks sent in their dues for the Delian League, instead of going to a neutral island, the money went to Athens. Pericles was not just using the money to support the league. He was rebuilding Athens with the funds. The rest of the Greek cities were unhappy, yet when they tried to withdraw from the League, Pericles harshly punished them.

Pericles [65]

In 451 BCE, Cimon sailed two hundred ships to seize Cyprus from the Persians. Cimon was killed, but the Greeks won. The war with Persia ended with the Callias Peace Treaty. Persia promised not to enter the Aegean Sea or try to retake Ionia. The Greeks gave Cyprus back to Persia and pledged not to attack North Africa or Anatolia. The Callias Peace Treaty lasted for thirty years.

Greece was still not at peace. Athens and Sparta had resumed their former animosity. Sparta led the Peloponnesian League, a rival of the Delian League. The First Peloponnesian War erupted in 460 BCE, pitting Athens against Corinth, Sparta, and other cities on the Peloponnese Peninsula. Athens had an impressive navy, but its army was no match for the Peloponnese forces. Sparta attacked Boeotia, north of Athens, and won the Battle of Tanagra. Athens sailed around the Peloponnese, attacking the coastal cities. Eventually, the First Peloponnesian War ended with the Thirty Years' Peace treaty in 445 BCE.

Only fourteen years passed before Sparta instigated the Second Peloponnesian War (431-404 BCE) by raiding the farms around Athens. Pericles knew the Spartans were trying to lure the Athenians into a land battle. Instead of fighting, he brought the rural people inside Athens and arranged for grain shipments from Egypt to feed everyone. He then established a naval blockade, cutting off sea trade to the Peloponnese.

However, the grain shipments brought rats, which spread a plague to the overcrowded city of Athens. The disease began with headaches, fever, and eye inflammation, then progressed to coughing, vomiting, violent diarrhea, and skin lesions. Tissue death caused people's fingers and toes to turn black and fall off. One-third of the city died, including Pericles. On the bright side, the Spartans evacuated the area, terrified of the plague. Ironically, the Athenian blockade kept ships from Egypt away from the Peloponnese; thus, the plague did not spread there.

Eventually, the plague burned out, and Athens resumed raiding the Peloponnese ports while building forts on the peninsula. Sparta bombarded the Athenian fort at Pylos; however, the Athenians surprised everyone by thrashing the Spartans. Their epic win filled them with confidence. They *could* win a land battle! When the Spartans commandeered Athens' silver mines in Thrace, Athens fought them in the heated Battle of Amphipolis. Sparta technically won but returned the silver mines to Athens in exchange for hostages.

While the Greek wars raged, its philosophers debated knowledge, reality, and truth. Socrates used a question-and-answer format to help his students navigate complex issues. Socrates explained he did not have all the answers, calling it "simple ignorance." Yet, "double ignorance" — someone who knows nothing but thinks he knows everything—was worse. A person like this was a "double fool." People lacking self-reflection and critical thinking skills were useless. "The unexamined life is not worth living!" Socrates insisted.

The leaders of Athens believed Socrates was instilling dangerous ideas in his students' minds. He faced trial for corrupting Athens's youth and for introducing "new spiritual things." Socrates criticized the Greek gods: "They lie, steal, and cheat on their spouses! How can we humans be moral if our gods are not?" However, Socrates was not an atheist. He believed in a good, wise, and perfect divine being. He spoke of a "daimonion," a guiding voice that warned him against certain actions.

The court convicted Socrates on both counts and ordered him to die by drinking hemlock.

Socrates' forced suicide [66]

Plato was a student and close companion of Socrates. He preserved Socrates' teachings through his *Dialogues*, a collection of texts in which Socrates discusses philosophy. Plato established the Academy around 387 BCE, where scholars met to debate and listen to lectures on philosophy, mathematics, astronomy, and politics.

In his "Theory of Forms," Plato explained that our understanding of reality is only a reflection of what is real. He compared it to living in a cave where people cannot see the sun, only the shadows on the cave walls. Most people fail to realize that the shadows are reflections of actual reality. What if someone got out of the cave? Plato explained what would happen:

> "He will be able to see the sun, and not mere reflections of him and he will contemplate him as he is. He will then argue that this is he who gives the seasons and the years and is the guardian of all that is in the visible world, and in a certain way the cause of all things."[7]

---

[7] Plato, *The Republic*, Book VII, trans. Benjamin Jowett (Daniel C. Stevenson, Web Atomics). http://classics.mit.edu/Plato/republic.9.viii.html.

Hippias, who debated with Plato in his *Dialogues*, was a philosopher who could discuss a wide range of topics, including astronomy, history, and mathematics. He discovered the geometric quadratrix, the intersection of a rotating line and a line moving parallel to itself. Hippias would attend the Olympic Games and invite people to choose any topic, then give a speech on that topic without advance preparation. Hippias complained that the concept of right and wrong was in constant flux as society changed. He argued that an unchanging "natural law" has always existed. Good is always good. Evil is always evil.

Plato's student Aristotle believed that an eternal, unchanging "unmoved mover" existing outside of time and space set the universe in motion. Aristotle taught the principle of deduction: if a premise is true, a conclusion based on that premise is also correct. For instance, a cat is a mammal (premise); thus, all lions are mammals (deduction). By contrast, induction makes a presumption based on observed fact. It may or may not be true. For example, one could see geese flying overhead (observed fact) and make the induction that all geese fly south for the winter.

Hippocrates, the "Father of Medicine," was from the island of Kos. At that time, people thought disease was a punishment from the gods. However, Hippocrates believed that lifestyle, diet, and environmental factors caused disease. He introduced clinical diagnosis, such as checking a patient's pain level, temperature, pulse, and range of motion. He also analyzed a patient's urine and bowel movements to determine their illness.

Before and during Greece's Golden Age, its city-states had a variety of government systems. A few had kings (Sparta had two at a time), some had a council, some had early forms of democracy, and some had a tyrant who came to power by popular support or through force and ruled with absolute power. A few cities experimented with several political systems. General Pericles reformed Athens's constitution and governmental structure to "the rule of the many instead of the few." He wanted Athens to be a model of democracy. Pericles pressed for equal justice for everyone and for all classes to serve in government. He paid working-class citizens for jury duty so they could afford to take time off from work.

Athens's Erechtheion temple with Caryatid pillars [67]

After Xerxes burned the Acropolis in Athens in 480 BCE, Pericles rebuilt its walls and temples. The Parthenon, a temple to Athena, had a thirty-eight-foot statue of the goddess covered with gold sheet, with an ivory face and arms. A second breathtaking temple to Athena was the Erechtheion. It has caryatid pillars in the shape of beautiful young women, each one different.

Greece's sculptures in its Golden Age displayed emotion and lively movement. The *Hermes of Praxiteles* sculpture in the Temple of Hera at Olympia portrays the baby Dionysus in Hermes's arms. Hermes stands with his weight on one leg in the "contrapposto" pose popular in Greece's Classical period.

Greece's Golden Age left a lasting legacy of democracy, philosophy, art, and science that continues to influence contemporary thought, governance, and culture.

Hermes holding Dionysius. [68]

# Chapter 9: Ancient Rome

This final chapter unfolds the formative stages of ancient Rome, beginning with its foundational story of Romulus and Remus, where myth and history intertwine. What influence did the Etruscans have on ancient Roman culture, governance, and architecture? Why did the Romans abandon their monarchy for a republic? What triggered early struggles between the social classes—the patricians and plebeians? How did Rome's initial territorial expansions and legal developments like the Twelve Tables play out? Let's examine how these foundational elements laid the groundwork for Rome's future dominance.

The legend of Romulus, the founder of Rome, begins with his ancestor Aeneas, a member of Troy's royal family. When the Greeks destroyed Troy (circa 1200 BCE), Aeneas escaped with his son and father. Along with other Trojan survivors, Aeneas experienced hair-raising adventures and adversities but finally settled in central Italy. Aeneas married Lavinia, the daughter of King Latinus of the Latin tribe.

Twelve generations later, his descendant Numitor was king of the Latin-Trojan coalition. Numitor's brother Amulius staged a coup, sent Numitor into exile, and forced Numitor's daughter, Rhea Silvia, to become a Vestal Virgin (he did not want her to have children). However, Rhea Silvia conceived twins during an eclipse, from being raped by the god Mars, she said. Furious, Amulius locked her in a tower and told his guard to drown the babies in the river.

But the guard did not have the heart to kill the boys. Instead, he put their basket in the river and let it float downstream. A wolf found the basket that had washed ashore with the crying twins. Her pups had died, so she suckled the boys from her swollen teats. Later, a shepherd found the babies and took them home to his wife to raise.

Romulus and Remus with the wolf in this statue from Brussels's Maison de la Louve [69]

When the twins grew up, they encountered their grandfather, Numitor, who was in exile. When the shepherd told Numitor how he found the infant boys by the river, Numitor realized they were his long-lost grandsons. The teens killed Amulius and restored their grandfather to his throne. Then, they set off to build their own city by the Tiber River, in the land of seven hills where their basket had landed when they were infants.

However, the young men quarreled over which hill to build on and which of them should be king. In the heat of the moment, Romulus killed his brother. He instantly regretted the fratricide, dissolving into tears. However, with his small band of men, he set to work building Rome and invited people in the surrounding areas to come live in his city. "Everyone will be a citizen, regardless of social status," he said. "Yes, even if you are a former slave, you can be a citizen in my city."

Rome's expansion efforts began at its inception. Romulus attracted several thousand young men to his new city, but they needed wives. The neighboring cities were unwilling to arrange marriages with this unknown upstart and his motley crew. So, Romulus devised a plan to abduct women for his people to marry. He threw a religious festival and invited the neighboring Sabines to come. He served strong wine to the Sabine men. When the Sabine men fell over drunk, the Romans stole their young women.

Once they sobered up, the Sabines demanded their women back, but Romulus refused to give them up. The men from the two Sabine cities who had attended the festival attacked Rome but failed to retrieve their women. So, they traveled around the Sabine lands, recruiting support. This took months, and during this time, many of the Sabine women had become pregnant.

When the two armies lined up to face each other, the women ran into the gap between the Romans and the Sabines. They turned toward the Romans and said, "Husbands! Stop fighting against our fathers and brothers!"

Then, they swirled around toward the Sabines and pleaded, "Fathers! We are pregnant with your grandchildren! Will you leave them fatherless? Please, don't fight because of us!"

The men on both sides wept at the women's pleas and put away their swords and spears. They formed a united Roman-Sabine kingdom led by co-rulers: Romulus and King Tatius of the Sabines. Five years later, an unknown assailant killed Tatius, leaving Romulus as the sole king of both lands.

Early Rome was home to diverse ethnicities, including Trojans, Latins, Greeks, Etruscans, and Sabines. The Etruscans were a neighboring civilization in central Italy. Although some Etruscans joined Romulus's new city, most Etruscans were Rome's adversaries, and war between them occasionally flared up. Rome conquered the Etruscans and the other tribes of central Italy by 264 BCE.

Rome's fifth king, Lucius Tarquinius Priscus, was the son of a Corinthian Greek and an Etruscan woman. He moved to Rome, where his pleasant and helpful personality made him a favorite of King Marcius. Rome did not have hereditary kings yet, so when Marcius died, the senators elected Tarquinius as king around 616 BCE. An impressive military commander, he expanded Rome's territory in central Europe, taking control of Latin, Etruscan, and Sabine territories.

Lucius Tarquinius Priscus built the Circus Maximus stadium for gladiator games (adopted from the Etruscans) and chariot races using Etruscan engineering techniques, including the arch and the tunnel vault.

For waste removal, he built the Cloaca Maxima, one of Europe's first advanced sewer systems.

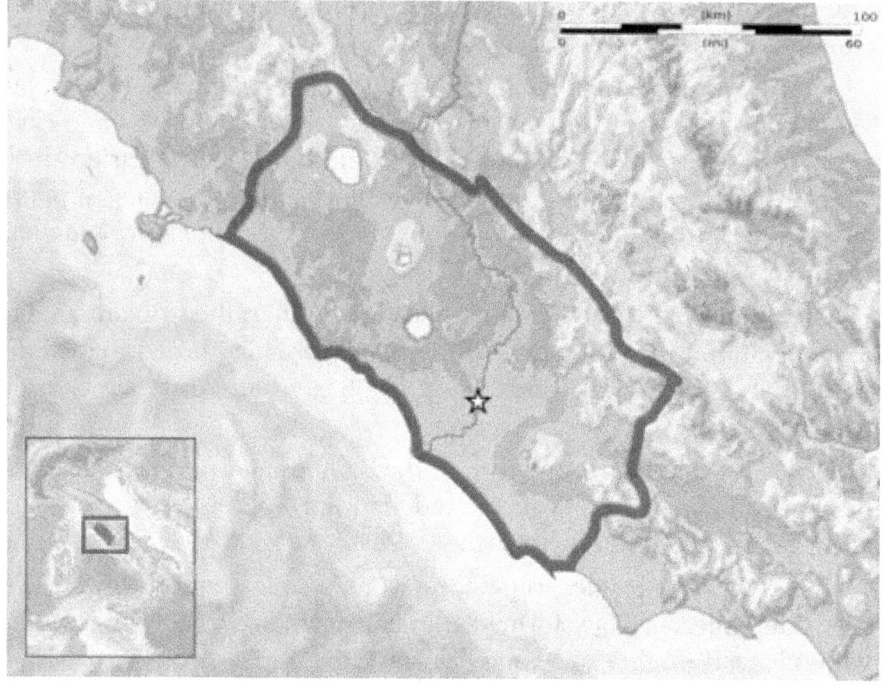

Rome's territory in its late monarchy [70]

Rome adapted the Etruscan alphabet into the Latin alphabet, the prototype for the alphabet used in most European countries today. The Etruscan alphabet descended from the Greek alphabet, which was based on the Phoenician alphabet. Rome also adopted Etruscan methods of foreseeing the future, such as haruspicy—examining animal intestines—and interpreting thunder and lightning.

Lucius Tarquinius Priscus had an enslaved woman, the widow of a Latin prince he killed in battle. He thought her son (and probably his), Servius Tullius, was brighter and had better omens than his legitimate sons, so he named Tullius as his heir. Meanwhile, the two sons of the former king Marcius, seething that they had been passed over for the throne, arranged for Tarquinius's murder. After Tarquinius's brutal end, his wife Queen Tanaquil manipulated events so that Servius Tullius became the regent for her two sons until they were old enough to rule.

However, Tullius never gave up the throne. He took Rome's first census, which counted about 80,000 citizens. He was a revolutionary, giving the working-class plebeians the right to vote and suggesting that the

Romans free their slaves—even grant them citizenship. Tullius was a hero to Rome's working people but a threat to the aristocratic patricians, the ruling class. Queen Tanaquil's son Tarquin plotted with the senators to overthrow Tullius. The conspirators murdered Tullius, and the Senate elected Tarquin as Rome's next king.

Within weeks, the senators realized they had made an abysmal mistake. King Tarquin the Proud was a villainous ruler, assassinating or exiling anyone who dared question him. He suppressed the Senate's power, and his killing spree even included his family members.

His son, Sextus Tarquinius, was equally evil. Tarquin's relative, Collatinus, had a beautiful wife named Lucretia. When Sextus tried to seduce Lucretia, she spurned his advances, so he raped her. Lucretia's husband and father were fighting in the army, but she messaged them to come home and bring two witnesses.

One witness was Brutus, the nephew of King Tarquin. He hated his uncle, who had killed his brother and father. Lucretia told the men what had happened and then pleaded, "Swear to me! Promise you will avenge what Sextus had done!"

Then, she pulled a knife from her robe and stabbed herself in the chest. Her father and husband screamed, collapsing in grief. But Brutus yanked the knife from her body and held it high. Drops of blood fell to the floor as he cried, "I swear! I will avenge Lucretia! Who is with me?"

The Oath of Brutus, by François-Joseph Navez [71]

All the men in the room held their daggers in the air and swore, "We will rid Rome of its kings!"

They carried Lucretia's bloodstained body to the Forum. "Look what Sextus Tarquinius has done to a virtuous wife and daughter!" they told the senators.

The senators gathered, horrified. An uproar arose from the growing crowd. In a fury, they vowed to overthrow the royal family: "We will end this reign of terror! No more tyranny! No more kings!"

In 509 BCE, Rome's senators voted to abolish the monarchy and establish a republic—a new form of government. "Instead of a king, we'll elect two consuls to rule together for a one-year term," they determined.

Brutus and Collatinus, Lucretia's husband, were Rome's first two consuls. The king and his sons fled Rome, desperately trying to get the Etruscans and Latins to support them in retaking the city. Tarquin still had supporters inside Rome, even the two sons of Brutus and his brothers-in-law. In a gruesome ritual, the conspirators killed a man and, touching his intestines, swore they would restore King Tarquin to his throne. A servant saw the grisly scene and reported it. Agonized, Brutus had no choice but to order his sons' execution.

In the new Roman Republic, the two elected consuls also served as commanders-in-chief of the military. Why two? If the Republic was at war, and it usually was, one man could lead the military while the other took care of administrative duties. If one man was too extreme, the other consul could veto his decisions. After his one-year term, a consul usually had to wait ten years before being reelected.

The Centuriate Assembly, made up of the military, voted for the consuls and other head leaders. One hundred soldiers formed a century, which got one vote in the elections. The consuls appointed the senators. In Rome's monarchy, the senators' chief function was to elect and advise the king. In the Republic, they passed new laws and controlled the budget. As the Republic rapidly grew, the Senate also focused on foreign policy.

To balance the military Centuriate Assembly, Rome later added an Assembly of Tribes, which represented geographical regions. It made laws, judged serious crimes, and elected certain magistrates. These included consuls, military commanders, and other top leadership positions, all serving one-year terms.

As the Romans thoughtfully developed their new Republic, they implemented checks and balances to keep one man or one group from having too much power or abusing power. These included elections, separation of powers, term limits, vetoes, impeachments, and quorum requirements. In the event of a crisis, the Senate could appoint a dictator for a term of up to six months. A dictator could make swift decisions without having to wait for the usual checks and balances. However, once the crisis was over, the dictator's term ended.

In the "Conflict of the Orders," beginning around 500 BCE, the plebeians—farmers, craftspeople, construction workers, and shopkeepers—struggled for political power. Rome's aristocratic landowners (patricians) held all the power in Rome's early days. They were the consuls, the senators, and the magistrates. As time passed, the plebeians demanded a voice in the government.

Initially, the patricians disregarded the pleas of the working-class people. The upper classes wanted to maintain the status quo. However, the plebeians had a secret weapon: *Secessio plebis*, or plebeian withdrawal. The patricians relied on the plebeians to farm, fight in the military, sell goods in the shops, and construct temples and amphitheaters. So, the plebeians all went on strike. They closed their shops, left their farms and building sites, and even abandoned the military outposts, heading to the countryside for a vacation.

The plebeian soldiers went on strike. [73]

It worked. The patricians could not function without the support of the plebeians. They were ready to come to the table and discuss the plebeians' grievances, which sounded something like this: "You pass new laws but don't inform us! Then, you arrest us for breaking a law we had no idea existed. You're also forcing us off the land on which we have been tenant farmers for centuries. You're bringing in all these prisoners-of-war as slaves and replacing us. Where are we supposed to live? When we cannot find work in the towns, you beat us and imprison us because we can't pay our debts!"

Rome established the Plebeian Assembly in 494 BCE, which could propose laws to the Senate and veto laws supported by the patricians. It addressed inequalities and grievances and eventually became a key political force. The Plebeian Assembly elected tribunes who protected the plebeians from the patricians' abuse of power.

In 450 BCE, twelve bronze tablets displaying the Law of the Twelve Tables were erected in the Forum in response to plebeian demands for written laws. This was Rome's first codified law system, a standard code for everyone. It put into writing early unwritten laws responding to legal questions such as family law, property issues, personal injury, and impiety.

Temple of Hera in Campania, Italy, built circa 460 BCE[73]

The Law of the Twelve Tables even addressed Rome's exceptional road system. Rome was constantly building roads during its Republic era as it conquered new territories, creating a network of roads led from all points in Italy to Rome. Rome financed the construction of these roads, but the law stipulated that the provinces had to maintain the roads that passed through their territory and that the roads had to be at least eight feet wide.

Before Rome's founding, Romulus's ancestors, the Latins and Trojans, had formed the Latin League, comprising about thirty cities, to defend themselves against mutual enemies. The league considered the Etruscans its greatest threat. Rome joined the Latin League in its early days, and the union persevered through Rome's monarchy period. When Rome became a Republic, it renewed its alliance with the cities in the league. In the *Foedus Cassianum*, the members vowed to fight together against common enemies, with an equal split of the spoils of war. Roman generals would lead their coalition armies. The Latin League was an almost unstoppable power.

In 458 BCE, the Aequi mountain tribe, located east of Rome, launched an attack on Rome's territories. Rome rose to the occasion and subdued the Aequi, but they attacked again months later. Rome decided it was time to put a temporary dictator into action. Cincinnatus, a former public servant, had retired to his farm in the countryside, but he was the one the Senate recommended. Although nominated for a six-month term, he trounced the Aequi in just over two weeks, resigned his dictatorship, and went back to his farm.

Ten years later, the Aequi allied with the Volsci people south of Rome. The coalition outnumbered Rome's army in the 446 BCE Battle of Corbio. The Romans split their army and circled around to the flanks of the Volsci-Aequi forces. Although the Romans won the battle, they lost six thousand men. Over the next sixty years, allied with the Latin League, the Romans finally subdued the Volski and Aequi, trounced the Etruscans, and blocked the Celtic invasion from the north.

Still, the Romans and Latins quarreled. In 338 BCE, Rome dissolved the Latin League and absorbed all the Latin cities into its Republic.

Once it controlled central Italy, Rome focused on the south. Centuries earlier, the Greeks had established colonies in southern Italy. In 280 BCE, Roman ships sailed into the Gulf of Taranto in southern Italy, and the Greeks promptly sank five of them. Rome declared war, and the Greeks asked King Pyrrhus of Epirus in northern Greece to help them. Pyrrhus had dreams of building an empire. This might be his chance!

Pyrrhus lacked resources, but he had wealthy relatives ruling Egypt, Macedonia, and the Middle East. He borrowed funds, military men, cavalry, and war elephants and sailed to Italy. Pyrrhus defeated the Romans in his first two battles but lost so many men that they were "pyrrhic victories," costing him more than what he won. He lost the third battle and sailed home in 275 BCE. Rome swallowed all of southern Italy, and by 270 BCE, it controlled the entire Italian peninsula.

# Conclusion

What did these ancient civilizations have in common, and what set them apart? How did they contribute to human progress? When faced with challenges, how did their responses shape their trajectories and legacies?

One commonality was learning to write. The Sumerians used simple pictographs by 3500 BCE, which developed into cuneiform symbols. Other civilizations adapted cuneiform, including the Hittites, Assyrians, and Persians. The Indus Valley Civilization's script shared similarities with Proto-Elamite, a script that evolved from Uruk's cuneiform. The Egyptians developed pictographs that evolved into hieroglyphics and influenced the early Greek scripts, which impacted the Roman alphabet. Around 1250 BCE, people in China's Shang dynasty began carving inscriptions on bones and shells. These characters influenced other East Asian scripts and evolved over the millennia into the modern Chinese writing system.

These civilizations all originated as herders or farmers who began building cities and evolved into complex societies with social hierarchies, extensive trade networks, and advanced technologies. They interacted with other civilizations and shared innovations. They were all warlike, determined to take more territory and expand their empires. The interconnectedness of these societies through trade, warfare, and cultural exchange illustrates early globalization.

Although their development followed a standard trajectory, their cultures were diverse. For instance, Sumerian cuneiform, Egyptian hieroglyphics, the Greek alphabet, and Chinese characters were all distinct writing systems. These civilizations had different religious systems, unique art forms, and varied philosophies. When conquering other lands, the Assyrians used shock and terror to subdue conquered people. Cyrus the Great took a more enlightened approach, using diplomacy and religious tolerance.

A common threat to these ancient civilizations was environmental changes, which either spelled disaster or inspired innovation and adaptation. The Sumerian culture burst on the scene after flooding destroyed the Ubaid city of Ur, and Eridu fell to drought and sandstorms. The Sumerians successfully rebuilt these cities, which continued to thrive for centuries, thanks to improved weather conditions and advanced technology for flood management and irrigation. Egypt's innovative farming techniques took advantage of the annual Nile flooding. The Hittite Empire and the Mycenaean civilization perished during the Bronze Age collapse, undone by a mega-drought, earthquakes, war, and disrupted sea trade. Climate change, like drought and desertification, also triggered the Indus Valley civilization's fall. Earthquakes that shifted rivers disrupted farming and river trade. However, in China, astute flood control helped Yu the engineer save the day and become the first emperor of the Xia dynasty.

Whether short or long-lived, these ancient civilizations contributed to our modern structures and ideologies. The Roman Republic was the foundation for modern democracy. Classical Greek philosophy shaped Roman politics and continues to influence our thinking today. The Persian Empire pioneered an administrative system that influenced the Roman Empire and today's governmental systems.

Through innovations in writing, technology, art, architecture, governance, and philosophy, these civilizations continue to impact us today.

# Here's another book by Enthralling History that you might like

## Free limited time bonus

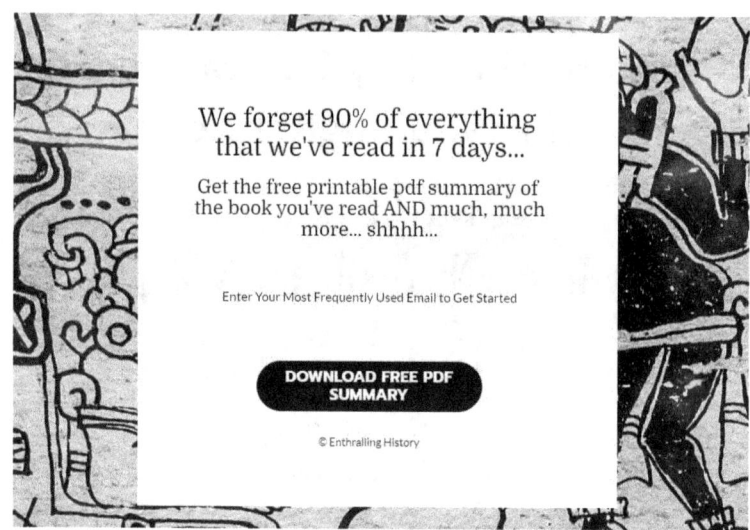

Stop for a moment. We have a free bonus set up for you. The problem is this: we forget 90% of everything that we read after 7 days. Crazy fact, right? Here's the solution: we've created a printable, 1-page pdf summary for this book that you're reading now. All you have to do to get your free pdf summary is to go to the following website: https://livetolearn.lpages.co/enthrallinghistory/

### Or, Scan the QR code!

Once you do, it will be intuitive. Enjoy, and thank you!

# Bibliography

Africanus, Sextus Julius. "The king lists of Africanus." Peter Lundström, 2011. Accessed May 19, 2025. https://pharaoh.se/africanus-king-list.

Barchiesi, Alessandro, and Walter Scheidel. *The Oxford Handbook of Roman Studies*. Oxford University Press, 2010.

Beate, Dignas, and Engelbert Winter. *Rome and Persia in Late Antiquity. Neighbours and Rivals*. Cambridge University Press, 2007.

Bertman, Stephen. *Handbook to Life in Ancient Mesopotamia*. Oxford University Press, 2005.

Boatwright, Mary T., Daniel J. Gargola, Noel Lenski, Richard J. A. Talbert. *The Romans: From Village to Empire: A History of Rome from Earliest Times to the End of the Western Empire*. Oxford University Press, November 22, 2011.

Brosius, Maria. *A History of Ancient Persia: The Achaemenid Empire*. Wiley Blackwell, 2020.

Castleden, Rodney. *The Knossos Labyrinth: A New View of the 'Palace of Minos' at Knossos*. Routledge, 2012.

Clements, Jonathan. *The First Emperor of China*. Sutton Publishing, 2007.

Clogg, Richard. *A Concise History of Greece*. Cambridge University Press, 2021.

Dalley, Stephanie. *Myths from Mesopotamia: Creation, the Flood, Gilgamesh, and Others*. Oxford University Press, 2008.

Dio, Cassius. *Roman History*. Translated by H. B. Foster. Published in Vol. I of the Loeb Classical Library edition, Macmillan Publishers, 1914. https://penelope.uchicago.edu/Thayer/E/Roman/Texts/Cassius_Dio/1*.html.

Dunand, Françoise, and Christiane Zivie-Coche. *Gods and Men in Egypt: 3000 BCE to 395 CE*. Translated by David Lorton. Cornell University Press, 2004.

*Enuma Elish: The Seven Tablets of Creation*. Translated by Leonard William King, 1902. https://www.sacred-texts.com/ane/stc/index.htm.

*Eridu Genesis.* Translated by Thorkild Jacobson. Livius, last updated 2020. https://www.livius.org/sources/content/oriental-varia/eridu-genesis/

Fenby, Jonathan. *The Dragon Throne: China's Emperors from the Qin to the Manchu.* Quercus Publishing, Ltd., 2015.

Gardiner, Sir Alan. *Egypt of the Pharaohs.* University Press, 1979.

"Gilgamesh and Aga." *The Electronic Text Corpus of Sumerian Literature,* Faculty of Oriental Studies, University of Oxford, 2000. https://etcsl.orinst.ox.ac.uk/section1/tr1811.htm.

Grayson, Albert Kirk. *Assyrian Rulers of the Early First Millennium BC: I (1114-859 BC).* University of Toronto Press, 2002. https://ia804706.us.archive.org/26/items/AssyrianRulersOfTheEarlyFirstMillenniumBc11114-859Bc/A.Kirk_Grayson_Assyrian_Rulers_of__Early_First_MBookFi.org.pdf.

Grayson, A. K. *Assyrian Rulers of the Early First Millennium BC II (858-745 BC).* University of Toronto Press, 1996.

Hoffner, Harry A. *Letters from the Hittite Kingdom: Writings from the Ancient World."* Society of Biblical Literature, 2009.

Kelder, Jorrit M. (2010). *The Kingdom of Mycenae: A Great Kingdom in the Late Bronze Age Aegean.* CDL Press, 2010.

Kenoyer, Jonathan Mark. *Ancient Cities of the Indus Valley Civilization.* Oxford University Press, 1998.

Kuhrt, Amélie. *The Persian Empire: A Corpus of Sources from the Achaemenid Period.* Routledge, 2007.

Lazaridis, I, A. Mittnik, N. Patterson, S. Mallick, N. Rohland, S. Pfrengle, A. Furtwängler, et al. "Genetic Origins of the Minoans and Mycenaeans." *Nature* 548 (August 10, 2017): 214-18. https://doi.org/10.1038/nature23310.

Lewis, Mark Edward. *The Early Chinese Empires: Qin and Han.* Harvard University Press, 2007.

Livy. *The Rise of Rome: Books One to Five.* Oxford University Press, July 1, 2009.

Lupack, Susan. "Mycenaean Religion." *The Oxford Handbook of the Bronze Age Aegean,* edited by Eric H. Cline, 2012. https://doi.org/10.1093/oxfordhb/9780199873609.013.0020.

Martin, Thomas R. *Ancient Rome: From Romulus to Justinian.* Yale University Press, September 10, 2013.

Matyszak, Philip. *The Rise of the Hellenistic Kingdoms, 336-250 BC.* Pen & Sword Military, 2019.

Parpola, Asko. *The Roots of Hinduism: The Early Aryans and the Indus Civilization.* Oxford University Press, 2015.

Pinch, Geraldine. *Egyptian Mythology: A Guide to the Gods, Goddesses, and Traditions of Ancient Egypt.* Oxford University Press, 2002.

Plato. *The Republic.* Translated by Benjamin Jowett. Daniel C. Stevenson, Web Atomics. Accessed June 28, 2025.
http://classics.mit.edu/Plato/republic.9.viii.html.

Pollock, Susan. *Ancient Mesopotamia.* Cambridge University Press, 1999.

Pomeroy, Sarah B., Stanley M. Burstein, Walter Donlan, Jennifer Tolbert Roberts, David W. Tandy, and Georgia Tsouvala. *Ancient Greece: Politics, Society, and Culture.* Oxford University Press, 2020.

Possehl, Gregory L. *The Indus Civilization: A Contemporary Perspective.* AltaMira Press, 2002.

Raulwing, Peter. *The Kikkuli Text. Hittite Training Instructions for Chariot Horses in the Second Half of the 2nd Millennium B.C. and Their Interdisciplinary Context.* The Long Riders Guild Academic Foundation, 2009.
http://www.lrgaf.org/Peter_Raulwing_The_Kikkuli_Text_MasterFile_Dec_2009.pdf.

Rhodes, P. J. *Athenian Democracy* (Edinburgh Readings on the Ancient World). Oxford University Press, 2004.

Sima Qian, *Shiji, Records of the Grand Scribe.* Ulrich Theobold, 2010.
http://www.chinaknowledge.de/Literature/Historiography/shiji.html.

*Sumerian King List.* Translated by Jean-Vincent Scheil, Stephen Langdon, and Thorkild Jacobsen. Livius, last updated 2020.
https://www.livius.org/sources/content/anet/266-the-sumerian-king-list/#Translation.

*The Epic of Gilgamesh.* Translated by N. K. Sandars. Penguin Classics, 1960.

*The Great Inscription of Tukulti-Ninurta I.* Translated by Yigal Bloch, 2017.
https://omnika.org/texts/626.

"This Old Pyramid" Transcript. *NOVA.* PBS Airdate: February 4, 1997.
https://www.pbs.org/wgbh/nova/transcripts/1915mpyramid.html.

Waters, Matt. *Ancient Persia: A Concise History of the Achaemenid Empire, 550-330 BCE.* Cambridge University Press, 2014.

Weatherford, Jack. *Genghis Khan and the Making of the Modern World.* Broadway Books, 2004.

Xenophon. *Cyropaedia: The Education of Cyrus.* Translated by Henry Graham Dakyns. Project Gutenberg, last updated 2011.
https://www.gutenberg.org/files/2085/2085-h/2085-h.htm.

Zarghamee, Reza. *Discovering Cyrus: The Persian Conqueror Astride the Ancient World.* Mage Publishers, 2018.

# Image Sources

1. Labels of today's countries and seas added for context. Karl Musser, CC BY-SA 2.5 <https://creativecommons.org/licenses/by-sa/2.5>, via Wikimedia Commons; https://commons.wikimedia.org/wiki/File:Tigr-euph.png
2. ALFGRN CC BY-SA 2.0 <https://creativecommons.org/licenses/by-sa/2.0>, via Wikimedia Commons; https://commons.wikimedia.org/w/index.php?curid=78172134
3. Umma, CC BY-SA 3.0 <http://creativecommons.org/licenses/by-sa/3.0/>, via Wikimedia Commons; https://commons.wikimedia.org/wiki/File:Sumer_map.jpg
4. Louvre Museum, CC BY 3.0 <https://creativecommons.org/licenses/by/3.0>, via Wikimedia Commons: https://commons.wikimedia.org/wiki/File:P1150884_Louvre_Uruk_III_tablette_%C3%A9criture_pr%C3%A9cun%C3%A9iforme_AO19936_rwk.jpg
5. https://commons.wikimedia.org/wiki/File:Sumerian_26th_c_Adab.jpg
6. https://commons.wikimedia.org/wiki/File:The_White_Temple_%27E_at_Uruk,_3500-3000_BCE.jpg
7. Osama Shukir Muhammed Amin FRCP(Glasg), CC BY-SA 4.0 <https://creativecommons.org/licenses/by-sa/4.0>, via Wikimedia Commons: https://commons.wikimedia.org/wiki/File:Warka_mask_(cropped).jpg
8. LeastCommonAncestor, CC BY-SA 3.0 <https://creativecommons.org/licenses/by-sa/3.0>, via Wikimedia Commons: https://commons.wikimedia.org/wiki/File:Standard_of_Ur_-_War_-_Detail_Bottom_Left.jpg
9. https://commons.wikimedia.org/wiki/File:Seal_dedicated_to_Ur-Nammu_(III_Dynasty_Ur)_(Ancient_Seals_of_the_Near_East,_No._6)_(1940).jpg

10 Map zoomed in. Jeff Dahl, CC BY-SA 4.0 <https://creativecommons.org/licenses/by-sa/4.0>, via Wikimedia Commons: https://commons.wikimedia.org/wiki/File:Ancient_Egypt_map-en.svg

11 https://commons.wikimedia.org/wiki/File:Design_of_the_Abydos_token_glyphs_dated_to_3400-3200_BCE.jpg

12 Quibell,1898, pl. 13, CC BY-SA 4.0 <https://creativecommons.org/licenses/by-sa/4.0>, via Wikimedia Commons: https://commons.wikimedia.org/wiki/File:Narmer_Palette_verso.svg

13 Charles J. Sharp, CC BY-SA 3.0 <https://creativecommons.org/licenses/by-sa/3.0>, via Wikimedia Commons: https://commons.wikimedia.org/wiki/File:Saqqara_pyramid_ver_2.jpg

14 Photo zoomed in. lienyuan lee, CC BY 3.0 <https://creativecommons.org/licenses/by/3.0>, via Wikimedia Commons: https://commons.wikimedia.org/wiki/File:Bent_Pyramid_%E6%9B%B2%E6%8A%98%E9%87%91%E5%AD%97%E5%A1%94_-_panoramio.jpg

15 Walkerssk, CC0, via Wikimedia Commons: https://commons.wikimedia.org/wiki/File:Pyramids_in_Giza_-_Egypt.jpg

16 Petar Milošević, CC BY-SA 4.0 <https://creativecommons.org/licenses/by-sa/4.0>, via Wikimedia Commons: https://commons.wikimedia.org/wiki/File:Great_Sphinx_of_Giza_(%D8%A3%D8%A8%D9%88_%D8%A7%D9%84%D9%87%D9%88%D9%84).jpg

17 Diego Delso, CC BY-SA 4.0 <https://creativecommons.org/licenses/by-sa/4.0>, via Wikimedia Commons: https://commons.wikimedia.org/wiki/File:Templo_de_Karnak,_Luxor,_Egipto,_2022-04-03,_DD_170-172_HDR.jpg

18 Eternal Space, CC BY-SA 4.0 <https://creativecommons.org/licenses/by-sa/4.0>, via Wikimedia Commons: https://commons.wikimedia.org/wiki/File:Tefnut_(Goddess).png

19 https://commons.wikimedia.org/wiki/File:BD_Hunefer_cropped_1.jpg

20 Photo zoomed in; labels added. Avantiputra7, CC BY-SA 3.0 <https://creativecommons.org/licenses/by-sa/3.0>, via Wikimedia Commons: https://commons.wikimedia.org/wiki/File:Indus_Valley_Civilization,_Mature_Phase_(2600-1900_BCE).png

21 Mamoon Mengal, CC BY-SA 1.0 <https://creativecommons.org/licenses/by-sa/1.0>, via Wikimedia Commons: https://commons.wikimedia.org/wiki/File:Mohenjo-daro_Priesterk%C3%B6nig.jpeg

22 Saqib Qayyum, CC BY-SA 3.0 <https://creativecommons.org/licenses/by-sa/3.0>, via Wikimedia Commons: https://commons.wikimedia.org/wiki/File:Mohenjo-daro.jpg

23 Matsyameena, CC BY-SA 4.0 <https://creativecommons.org/licenses/by-sa/4.0>, via Wikimedia Commons: https://commons.wikimedia.org/wiki/File:Intaglio_seal_(H97-3433-7617-01)_Indus_Fish_symbol_.png

24 Gary Todd, CC0, via Wikimedia Commons: Commons: https://commons.wikimedia.org/wiki/File:Harappa_Indus_Valley_seal_with_fighting_scene.jpg

25 Ismoon (talk) 18:40, 21 February 2012 (UTC), CC0, via Wikimedia Commons: https://commons.wikimedia.org/wiki/File:Figure_between_two_tigers._Mold_of_Seal,_Indus_valley_civilization.jpg

26 Geoff Soper, CC BY-SA 4.0 <https://creativecommons.org/licenses/by-sa/4.0>, via Wikimedia Commons: https://commons.wikimedia.org/wiki/File:A_Punjab_Wheel,_India_c1919.jpg

27 Map zoomed in, labels added. Edited by w:nl:hanhil, Public domain, via Wikimedia Commons: https://commons.wikimedia.org/wiki/File:Levantine_Sea.jpg

28 cavorite https://www.flickr.com/photos/cavorite/, CC BY-SA 2.0 <https://creativecommons.org/licenses/by-sa/2.0>, via Wikimedia Commons: https://commons.wikimedia.org/wiki/File:Palace_of_Knossos.jpg

29 Mary Harrsch, CC BY-SA 4.0 <https://creativecommons.org/licenses/by-sa/4.0>, via Wikimedia Commons: Commons: https://commons.wikimedia.org/wiki/File:Linear_A_tablet_Clay_from_Chania.jpg

30 Zde, CC BY-SA 4.0 <https://creativecommons.org/licenses/by-sa/4.0>, via Wikimedia Commons: https://commons.wikimedia.org/wiki/File:Marine_Style,_Zakros,_1600-1450_BC,_AMH,_145043.jpg

31 https://commons.wikimedia.org/wiki/File:Knossos_Bull-Leaping_Fresco.jpg

32 Labels added. Ulamm 23:14, 20 January 2008 (UTC), CC BY-SA 3.0 <https://creativecommons.org/licenses/by-sa/3.0>, via Wikimedia Commons: https://commons.wikimedia.org/wiki/File:Peloponnisos-b2.png

33 William Neuheisel from DC, US, CC BY 2.0 <https://creativecommons.org/licenses/by/2.0>, via Wikimedia Commons: https://commons.wikimedia.org/wiki/File:Lions_Gate_at_Mycenae_(5228010382).jpg

34 Zde, CC BY-SA 4.0 <https://creativecommons.org/licenses/by-sa/4.0>, via Wikimedia Commons: https://commons.wikimedia.org/wiki/File:Linear_B_tablet,_AM_of_Mycenae,_201726.jpg

35 User:George E. Koronaios, CC BY-SA 4.0 <https://creativecommons.org/licenses/by-sa/4.0>, via Wikimedia Commons: https://commons.wikimedia.org/wiki/File:Mural_composition_from_the_Palace_of_Thebes_(14th-13th_c._B.C.)_at_the_Archaeological_Museum_of_Thebes_on_10_April_2019_(cropped).jpg

36 w:en:User:Gurdjieff (Lamassu Design), CC BY-SA 3.0 <https://creativecommons.org/licenses/by-sa/3.0>, via Wikimedia Commons: https://commons.wikimedia.org/wiki/File:Xia_dynasty.svg

37 僧盐, CC BY-SA 4.0 <https://creativecommons.org/licenses/by-sa/4.0>, via Wikimedia Commons: https://commons.wikimedia.org/wiki/File:%E7%BB%BF%E6%9D%BE%E7%9F%B3%E9%BE%99%E5%BD%A2%E5%99%A88.jpg

38 BabelStone, CC BY-SA 3.0 <https://creativecommons.org/licenses/by-sa/3.0>, via Wikimedia Commons: https://commons.wikimedia.org/wiki/File:Oracle_bones_at_Pitt_Rivers_Museum.jpg

39 Gary Todd, CC0, via Wikimedia Commons: https://commons.wikimedia.org/wiki/File:Shang_Chariot_Replica.jpg

40 Mary Harrsch, CC BY-SA 4.0 <https://creativecommons.org/licenses/by-sa/4.0>, via Wikimedia Commons: https://commons.wikimedia.org/wiki/File:Bronze_Bird-Shaped_Wine_Container_(Niao_Zun)_Shang_dynasty_12th-11th_century_BCE_China.jpg

41 Labels added. Territories_of_Dynasties_in_China.gif: Ian Kiu, CC BY-SA 3.0 <http://creativecommons.org/licenses/by-sa/3.0/>, via Wikimedia Commons; https://commons.wikimedia.org/wiki/File:Zhou_dynasty_1000_BC.png

42 Photo zoomed in. Gary Lee Todd, Ph.D., CC0, via Wikimedia Commons: https://commons.wikimedia.org/wiki/File:Eastern_Zhou_Jade_Ornament_04.jpg

43 Map zoomed in, labels added. Enyavar, CC BY-SA 4.0 <https://creativecommons.org/licenses/by-sa/4.0>, via Wikimedia Commons: https://commons.wikimedia.org/wiki/File:Ancient_Near_East_1300BC.svg

44 Bernard Gagnon, CC BY-SA 3.0 <https://creativecommons.org/licenses/by-sa/3.0>, via Wikimedia Commons: https://commons.wikimedia.org/wiki/File:Sphinx_Gate,_Hattusa_01.jpg

45 https://commons.wikimedia.org/wiki/File:Weather_God.jpg

46 https://commons.wikimedia.org/wiki/File:Modern_loose_interpretation_at_the_The_Pharaonic_Village_in_Cairo_of_a_Battle_scene_from_the_Great_Kadesh_reliefs_of_Ramses_II_on_the_Walls_of_the_Ramesseum.jpg

47 https://commons.wikimedia.org/wiki/File:Ashur_symbol_Nimrud.png

48 Lawson G. Stone, CC BY-SA 4.0 <https://creativecommons.org/licenses/by-sa/4.0>, via Wikimedia Commons; https://commons.wikimedia.org/wiki/File:Assyrian_King_Kills_a_Lion.jpg

49 Dosseman, CC BY-SA 4.0 <https://creativecommons.org/licenses/by-sa/4.0>, via Wikimedia Commons; https://commons.wikimedia.org/wiki/File:Antakya_Archaeological_Museum_Statue_of_Suppiluliuma_sept_2019_5792.jpg

50 https://commons.wikimedia.org/wiki/File:C%2BB-Siege-Fig3-AssyrianSiegeTower.PNG

51 User Chaldean on en.wikipedia, CC BY-SA 3.0 <http://creativecommons.org/licenses/by-sa/3.0/>, via Wikimedia Commons; https://commons.wikimedia.org/wiki/File:ShalmaneserIII.jpg

52 Map zoomed in. Nigyou, CC BY-SA 3.0 <https://creativecommons.org/licenses/by-sa/3.0>, via Wikimedia Commons: https://commons.wikimedia.org/wiki/File:Neo-Assyrian_map_824-671_BC.png

53 Photo zoomed in, labels added. Natural Earth, CC BY-SA 4.0 <https://creativecommons.org/licenses/by-sa/4.0>, via Wikimedia Commons; https://commons.wikimedia.org/wiki/File:Colorful_shaded_map_of_Middle_East.jpg

54 Original: User:SzajciEnglish: User: WillemBK, CC BY-SA 3.0 <https://creativecommons.org/licenses/by-sa/3.0>, via Wikimedia Commons https://commons.wikimedia.org/wiki/File:Median_Empire-en.svg:

55 Aneta Ribarska, CC BY-SA 3.0 <https://creativecommons.org/licenses/by-sa/3.0>, via Wikimedia Commons https://commons.wikimedia.org/wiki/File: Persepolis_carvings.JPG

56 Cyrus the Great, CC BY-SA 4.0 <https://creativecommons.org/licenses/by-sa/4.0>, via Wikimedia Commons: https://commons.wikimedia.org/wiki/File:At_the_British_Museum_2024_235.jpg

57 https://commons.wikimedia.org/wiki/File:Persepolis_Reconstruction_Apadana_Chipiez.jpg

58 Frank-Haf, CC BY-SA 4.0 <https://creativecommons.org/licenses/by-sa/4.0>, via Wikimedia Commons; https://commons.wikimedia.org/wiki/File:Darius_the_Great.jpg

59 Mohammad.m.nazari, CC BY-SA 4.0 <https://creativecommons.org/licenses/by-sa/4.0>, via Wikimedia Commons; https://commons.wikimedia.org/wiki/File: Unicorn_in_Apadana,_Shush,_Iran--2017-10.jpg

60 https://commons.wikimedia.org/wiki/File:Datis_fighting_Kallimachos_at_the_Battle_of_Marathon_in_the_Stoa_Poikile_(reconstitution).jpg

61 Original creator: MossmapsCorrections according to Oxford Atlas of World History 2002, The Times Atlas of World History (1989), Philip's Atlas of World History (1999) by पाटलिपुत्र, CC BY-SA 4.0 <https://creativecommons.org/licenses/by-sa/4.0>, via Wikimedia Commons: https://commons.wikimedia.org/wiki/File: Achaemenid_Empire_at_its_greatest_extent_according_to_Oxford_Atlas_of_World_History_2002.jpg

62 Photo zoomed in, labels added. Greece_location_map.svg: Lencer / derivative work: Uwe Dedering, CC BY-SA 3.0 <https://creativecommons.org/licenses/by-sa/3.0>, via Wikimedia Commons: https://commons.wikimedia.org/wiki/File: Greece_relief_location_map.jpg

63 Photo modified: labels added. Aegean_Sea_map_bathymetry-fr.svg: Eric Gaba (Sting - fr:Sting)derivative work: MinisterForBadTimes, CC BY-SA 3.0 <https://creativecommons.org/licenses/by-sa/3.0>, via Wikimedia Commons; https://commons.wikimedia.org/wiki/File:Thermopylae_%26_Artemisium_campaign_map.png

64 https://commons.wikimedia.org/wiki/File:Ship_dashed_against_ship,_till_the_Persian_Army_dead_strewed_the_deep_like_flowers.jpg

65 Vatican Museums, CC BY 3.0 <https://creativecommons.org/licenses/by/3.0>, via Wikimedia Commons: https://commons.wikimedia.org/wiki/File:Pericles_Pio-Clementino_Inv269_n4.jpg

66 Jacques-Louis David, CC0, via Wikimedia Commons; https://commons.wikimedia.org/wiki/File:The_Death_of_Socrates_MET_DT40.jpg

67 lensnmatter, CC BY 2.0 https://creativecommons.org/licenses/by/2.0>, via Wikimedia Commons: https://commons.wikimedia.org/wiki/File: Caryatids_of_Erechtheion_(20419658495).jpg

68 Photo zoomed in. Paolo Villa, CC BY-SA 4.0 <https://creativecommons.org/licenses/by-sa/4.0>, via Wikimedia Commons; https://commons.wikimedia.org/wiki/File:02_2020_Grecia_photo_Paolo_Villa_FO190025_(Museo_archeologico_di_Olimpia_-_Statua_Ermes_con_Dioniso_Bambino_scolpita_da_Prassitele,_Arte_pre_Ellenistica,_dettaglio_superiore).jpg

69 Photo zoomed in. Trougnouf, CC BY 4.0 <https://creativecommons.org/licenses/by/4.0>, via Wikimedia Commons: https://commons.wikimedia.org/wiki/File:Maison_de_la_Louve_(DSC_0377).jpg

70 © Sémhur / Wikimedia Commons: https://commons.wikimedia.org/wiki/File:Late_Roman_kingdom_map-blank.svg

71 https://commons.wikimedia.org/wiki/File:Fran%C3%A7ois-Joseph_Navez001.jpg

72 https://commons.wikimedia.org/wiki/File:Secessio_plebis.JPG

73 Norbert Nagel, CC BY-SA 3.0 <https://creativecommons.org/licenses/by-sa/3.0>, via Wikimedia Commons: https://commons.wikimedia.org/wiki/File:Hera_temple_II_-_Paestum_-_Poseidonia_-_July_13th_2013_-_04.jpg